THE TOTAL JAZZ GUITARIST

>> A Fun and Comprehensive Overview of Jazz Guitar Playing

JODY FISHER

Alfred, the leader in educational publishing,

and the National Guitar Workshop,

one of America's finest guitar schools, have joined

forces to bring you the best, most progressive

educational tools possible. We hope you will enjoy

this book and encourage you to look for

other fine products from Alfred and the

National Guitar Workshop.

Alfred Publishing Co., Inc.
16320 Roscoe Blvd., Suite 100
P.O. Box 10003
Van Nuys, CA 91410-0003
alfred.com

ISBN-10: 0-7390-3848-6 (Book & CD)
ISBN-13: 978-0-7390-3848-2 (Book & CD)

This book was acquired, edited and produced
by Workshop Arts, Inc., the publishing arm of
the National Guitar Workshop.
Nathaniel Gunod, acquisitions, managing editor
Burgess Speed, editor
Matthew Liston, assistant editor
Timothy Phelps, interior design
Ante Gelo, music typesetter
CD recorded at Studio 9, Ontario, CA

Cover guitar courtesy Gibson USA.

Table of Contents

About the Author 4

Introduction 5

Part 1: The Toolbox 6
Chapter 1: The Basics 6
    Standard Music Notation 6
    Essential Chords 8
    Pentatonic Scale Fingerings 9

Chapter 2: The Chromatic Scale 10

Chapter 3: The Major Scale 12
    Major Scale Construction 12
    The Circle of 4ths/5ths 13
    Horizontal Major Scale Fingerings 16
    One-Octave Vertical Fingerings 17
    Two-Octave Vertical Fingerings 18
    Learning and Practicing the Major Scales 19

Chapter 4: Melodic Patterns 23
    Creating Your Own Melodic Patterns 24

Chapter 5: Triads 26
    Major Triads 26
    Minor Triads 27
    Diminished Triads 28
    Augmented Triads 28
    Finding Triads on the Fretboard 29
    1st Inversion Triads 30
    2nd Inversion Triads 31

Chapter 6: Major Family Chords 32
    Major 6th Chords 32
    Major 7th Chords 33
    A Cool Way to Learn New Chords 33
    Extended Chords 35
    Major 9th Chords 36
    Major 13th Chords 36

Chapter 7: Minor Family Chords 37
    Minor 6th Chords 37
    Minor Add 9th Chords 37
    Minor 7th Chords 38
    Minor 9th Chords 38
    Minor 11th Chords 39
    Minor 13th Chords 39

Chapter 8: Dominant Family Chords 40
    Dominant 7th Chords 40
    Dominant 9th Chords 40
    Dominant 11th Chords 41
    Dominant 13th Chords 41

Chapter 9: Half-Diminished 7th and Full-
  Diminished 7th Chords 42
    Omitting Chord Tones 42

Chapter 10: Diatonic Harmony 43
    Harmonized Major Scales 43
    Diatonic Arpeggios of the Major Scale 45
    The Modes of the Major Scale 48

Chapter 11: Altered Chords 51
    Altered Dominant Chords 51
    Altered Major Chords 52
    Altered Minor Chords 52

Chapter 12: The Minor Scales 53
    The Harmonic Minor Scale 54
    The Melodic Minor Scale 55
    The Harmonized Minor Scales 56
    The Modes of the Minor Scales 58

Chapter 13: The ii–V7–I Progression 60
    Extending or Altering Chords 60
    Importance of the ii and V7 60
    Minor ii–V7–i Progressions 61

Chapter 14: Applying Neighbor Tones 62

Chapter 15: Altered Scales 64
    The Diminished Scale 64
    The Whole Tone Scale 66
    The Super Locrian Mode 67

Chapter 16: Turnarounds 68

Part 2: Learning Tunes 70

   Chapter 17: "I'm in the Mood for Love"...............71

      Learning the Melody 72

         I'm in the Mood for Love

           (Melody in Single Notes) 72

         I'm in the Mood for Love

           (Melody One Octave Higher) 74

      Working on the Changes 76

         I'm in the Mood for Love

           (Comping Example) 95

      Chord Melody Style...............................96

         I'm in the Mood for Love

           (Chord Melody) 98

      Learning to Improvise........................100

         I'm in the Mood for Love

           (Solo Using Only Arpeggio Tones) 104

         I'm in the Mood for Love

           ("Improvised" Solo) 110

   Chapter 18: "Over the Rainbow".........................112

      Over the Rainbow

         (Melody in Single Notes) 112

      Over the Rainbow

         (Comping Example) 113

      Over the Rainbow

         (Chord Melody) 114

      Over the Rainbow

         ("Improvised" Solo) 116

   Chapter 19: "Blue Moon" 118

      Blue Moon

         (Melody in Single Notes) 118

      Blue Moon

         (Comping Example) 120

      Blue Moon

         (Chord Melody) 121

      Blue Moon

         ("Improvised" Solo) 122

   Chapter 20: The Blues and Rhythm Changes.....124

      The Blues...124

      Rhythm Changes....................................126

   Conclusion 127

About the Author

Jody Fisher has worked professionally in virtually all styles of music during his career, from straight-ahead and contemporary jazz to rock 'n' roll, country and pop. For several years, he was a director of the National Guitar Workshop. He also taught Guitar and Jazz Studies at both the University of Redlands and Idyllwild School of Music and the Arts (ISOMATA). He is an active performer in the Southern California area, where he maintains a busy private teaching practice.

PHOTO BY LARRY LYTLE

Other instructional materials by Jody Fisher:

30-Day Guitar Workout (Alfred/National Guitar Workshop—Book #17867)

Chord and Scale Finder (Alfred/National Guitar Workshop—Book #14148)

Ear Training for the Contemporary Guitarist (Alfred/National Guitar Workshop—Book & CD #19370)

Jazz Guitar Christmas Solos (Alfred/National Guitar Workshop—Book & CD #14869)

Jazz Guitar Masterclass (with Joe Diorio, Mark Whitfield, Ron Escheté, Scott Henderson and Steve Khan) (Alfred/National Guitar Workshop—Book #14827)

Jazz Skills (National Guitar Workshop—Book & CD #07-1012)

Rhythm Guitar Encyclopedia (Alfred/National Guitar Workshop—Book & 2 CDs #14838)

Stand Alone Tracks: Smooth Jazz (Alfred/National Guitar Workshop—Book & CD #17808)

The Complete Jazz Method:

    Beginning Jazz Guitar (Alfred/National Guitar Workshop—Book & CD #14120)

    Intermediate Jazz Guitar (Alfred/National Guitar Workshop—Book & CD #14123)

    Mastering Jazz Guitar: Chord/Melody (Alfred/National Guitar Workshop—Book & CD #14126)

    Mastering Jazz Guitar: Improvisation (Alfred/National Guitar Workshop—Book & CD #14129)

The Guitar Mode Encyclopedia (Alfred/National Guitar Workshop—Book #4445)

Jazz Guitar Harmony (Alfred/National Guitar Workshop—Book & CD #20440)

The Art of Solo Guitar, Book 1 (National Guitar Workshop—Book & CD #07-1053)

The Art of Solo Guitar, Book 2 (National Guitar Workshop—Book & CD #07-1056)

I Used to Play Guitar (Alfred/National Guitar Workshop—Book & CD #22683)

Teaching Guitar (Alfred/National Guitar Workshop—Book & CD #22916)

Jazz Licks Encyclopedia (Alfred/National Guitar Workshop—Book & CD #19420)

Introduction

The idea behind *The Total Jazz Guitarist* is to show aspiring jazz guitarists the real-world skills and ideas that lead to jazz guitar mastery. No single book can fully train any artist—it takes many years of study, practice and experience before a player can become competent, much less develop a voice of his or her own.

Part I of this book (The Toolbox, page 6) is a comprehensive survey of the most important theoretical and technical aspects of jazz guitar. It starts with a brief review of guitar and notation basics. Then, from basic scale and triad construction, we move along to more advanced ideas. The commentary has been kept brief to make room for more musical examples.

In Part 2 (Learning Tunes, page 70), the ideas and techniques discussed in Part I are applied to actual *standards*, songs from the Great American Songbook (an informal collection of popular, Broadway and film songs that form the basic repertoire of jazz music). Each song is analyzed from four different perspectives:

1. Learning to play the tune in single notes in various *registers*, or ranges of pitch. This skill is essential when working with other "chordal" instruments like keyboards or a second guitar.

2. Treating the song harmonically by way of *comping* patterns. To "comp" is to accompany a melody or solo. Lots of different chord voicings are shown here as well.

3. Basic *chord melody* techniques. To play a "chord melody" is to play a song's melody and harmony, or accompaniment, simultaneously. The arrangements here are fairly easy, which should give the chord melody novice immediate access to this kind of playing.

4. Various ways a player can improvise over the song's chord changes.

This book can be used in a number of ways. If you are new to jazz, Part I can be used as an actual method. Simply begin on a chapter in which the material seems new to you and move on from there. If you have been playing for a while but are a little fuzzy in some areas, Part I can be used as a review. If you know most of the information in Part I, you may want to use it as a reference guide, or as a place to grab new chord voicings or arpeggio fingerings. If you want to jump right into the songs, go directly to Part 2.

Following is a list of books (all published by Alfred/National Guitar Workshop) that would make great companions to this volume. Working with these other sources will allow you to drill down a little deeper into the material presented here.

The Complete Jazz Guitar Method, consisting of:
   Beginning Jazz Guitar (#14120)
   Intermediate Jazz Guitar (#14123)
   Mastering Jazz Guitar: Chord/Melody (#14126)
   Mastering Jazz Guitar: Improvisation (#14129)

Also:
   Jazz Guitar Harmony (#20440)
   The Art of Solo Guitar, Books 1 and 2 (#07-1053/1056)
   Jazz Licks Encyclopedia (#19420)
   The Big Book of Jazz Guitar Improvisation (#21968)

Enjoy these studies.

Jody Fisher

 A compact disc is available with this book. Using the disc will help make learning more enjoyable and the information more meaningful. Listening to the CD will help you correctly interpret the rhythms and feel of each example. The symbol to the left appears next to each song or example that is performed on the CD. Example numbers are above the symbol. The track number below each symbol corresponds directly to the song or example you want to hear. Track 1 will help you tune to this CD.

PART I: The Toolbox

Chapter 1: The Basics

Most guitarists who want to study jazz have some experience with the basics of technique and theory. However, this chapter is a review of the general concepts you will need to use this book. You can refer to *The Total Acoustic Guitarist* by Frank Natter, Jr. (Alfred/National Guitar Workshop #24426) or *The Total Rock Guitarist* (Alfred/National Guitar Workshop #24423) by Tobias Hurwitz if you need further clarification of these concepts.

Standard Music Notation

Reading *standard music notation* is a necessary skill for anyone interested in learning to play jazz. Once you get the idea, you'll find that it's really easy, and then a whole world of instructional books and great music will open up for you.

Music is written on a *staff* (consisting of five lines and four spaces) in *treble clef* 𝄞 (also known as G clef). This clef encircles the 2nd line from the bottom and tells us that this line represents the note G (see example below).

From that reference note we can continue the *musical alphabet* (A–B–C–D–E–F–G; A–B–C, etc.) above and below the G line. *Ledger lines* are used for notes above and below the staff.

The Staff

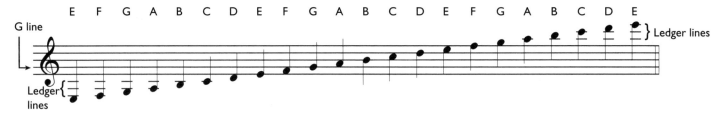

Accidentals

An *accidental* is a symbol that alters the pitch (which also refers to the "highness" or "lowness" in tone) of a note.

♯ = *Sharp*. Raises the pitch of a note by one *half step* (one fret).

♭ = *Flat*. Lowers the pitch of a note by one half step.

♮ = *Natural*. Returns a note to its original pitch.

Time Signatures, Measures and Bar Lines

Every piece has numbers at the beginning, called the *time signature*, that tell us how to count the time. The top number represents the number of beats or counts per *measure*. The bottom number represents the type of note receiving one count. Measures are groupings of beats separated by *bar lines*. The most common time signature, 𝄴, is shown below. In 𝄴 time, there are four beats per measure and the quarter note (♩) receives one beat.

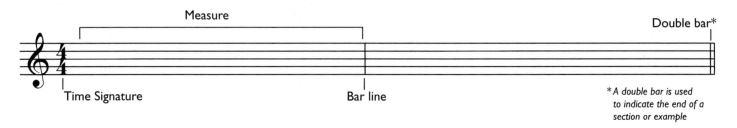

* A double bar is used to indicate the end of a section or example

The appearance of the note—the type of *notehead* or *stem* it has—tells you the duration, or *value*. *Rests* indicate silence. Here are the note and rest values:

| Whole rest 4 beats | Half rest 2 beats | Quarter rest 1 beat | Eighth rest ½ beat | Sixteenth rest ¼ beat |
| Whole note 4 beats | Half note 2 beats | Quarter note 1 beat | Eighth note ½ beat | Sixteenth note ¼ beat |

Tablature

Tablature, or TAB, is a system used for guitar and other fretted instruments. There are six lines that represent the strings (not notes). Numbers are placed on the lines; these numbers tell you what frets to play. Numbers under the TAB staff tell you which left-hand fingers to use. The top line represents the 1st string and the bottom line represents the 6th string. In this book, TAB is written below the corresponding standard music notation.

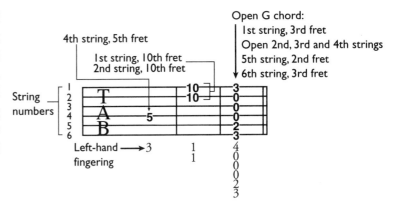

Chord Diagrams

A *chord* is three or more notes played at the same time. A *chord diagram,* which is oriented vertically, illustrates the fretboard and shows you the position, shape and fingering for a chord. To decipher a chord diagram, imagine that you are facing your guitar while it is resting on a guitar stand.

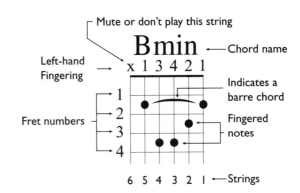

Scale Diagrams

Scale diagrams use similar indications as chord diagrams except that they are horizontal representations of the guitar neck as opposed to the vertical layout of the chord diagram. They can be used to illustrate different concepts but are most commonly used to display scale fingerings.

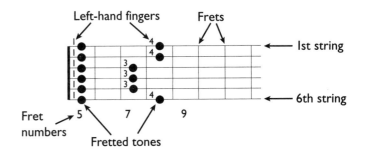

Essential Chords

You need to know the basic chords (most of which are *open* chords, which use one or more open strings). You also need to know the standard movable chord fingerings. If you don't know these chords, learn them well before proceeding.

Basic Chords

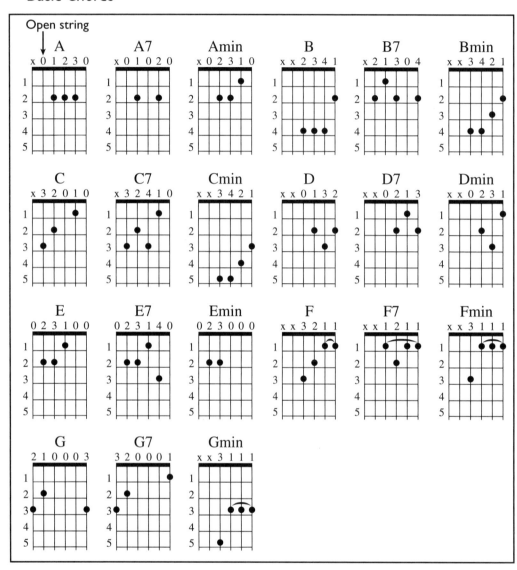

⌒ = Barre.
Use the same finger to fret more than one note by laying it flat across the strings.

Movable Chords

To the right are the *movable chord* fingerings with the *root* (note upon which the chord is built and from which it receives its name) on the 6th string. Notice there are no fret numbers. This is because they are "movable"—they can be moved anywhere on the fretboard, and wherever you place the root, that is the name of the chord. For example, if you place the minor fingering at the 5th fret (the note on the 5th fret of the 6th string is A) the chord becomes an A Minor chord.

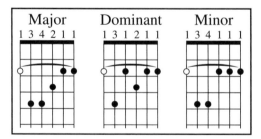

O = Root

To the right are the fingerings with the root on the 5th string.

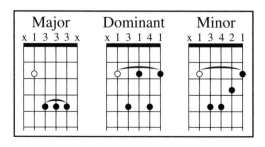

Pentatonic Scale Fingerings

It is helpful to have some experience improvising in a very basic blues or rock context. You should be familiar with the following minor and major *pentatonic scale* fingerings. The pentatonic scale is a five-note scale. The *major pentatonic* scale consists of scale degrees 1–2–3–5–6 and the *minor pentatonic* scale consists of scale degrees 1–♭3–4–5–♭7. If you understand this, great. If not, that's alright; study the pages that follow and refer back to this.

C Major Pentatonic Scale

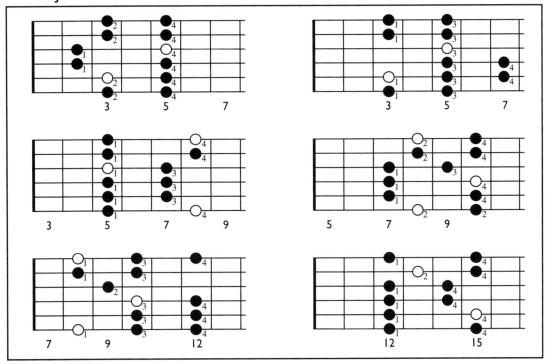

C Minor Pentatonic Scale

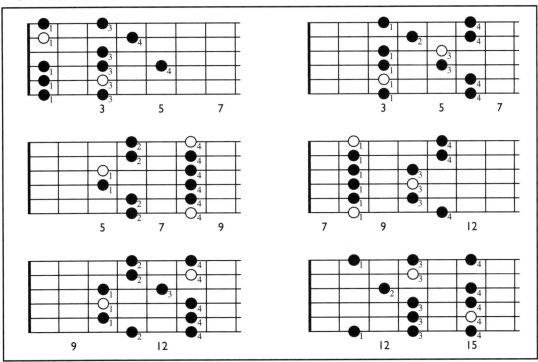

Chapter 2: The Chromatic Scale

Note: If you are exploring jazz for the first time, you should go through the rest of Part 1 in a slow, methodical way. The material here works its way from very basic concepts to the much more complex. Much of your success as a competent jazz guitarist depends on how well-versed you are in the fundamentals. Part 2 of this book assumes that you have most of this information in your head and under your fingers.

If you have been a student of jazz for a while and are familiar with most of the concepts in Part 1, by all means, jump right into Part 2.

If you are somewhere in between the two, there is no reason why you cannot work in Part 2 using the first part as more of a reference guide when you run across unfamiliar concepts.

In our Western music system, we have 12 tones that are repeated over and over, spanning many *octaves* (an octave is the distance between two pitches with the same name). We call this set of tones the *chromatic scale* (a *scale* is a set of notes that divides the octave into a specific pattern of whole and half steps). All of the notes in the chromatic scale are one *half step* away from each other, or the distance of one fret on the guitar. Two half steps, or the distance of two frets on the guitar, equal a *whole step*.

Chromatic Scale

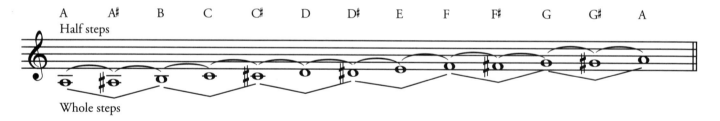

There are quite a few ways to play a chromatic scale on the guitar. Probably the most obvious way is to simply play every note ascending along any individual string. Following are chromatic scales beginning on each open string. Play these scales until the notes sound even, in terms of volume and tone.

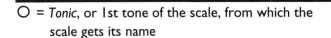
○ = *Tonic*, or 1st tone of the scale, from which the scale gets its name

E Chromatic Scale

A Chromatic Scale

D Chromatic Scale

G Chromatic Scale

B Chromatic Scale

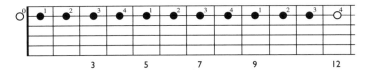

E Chromatic Scale

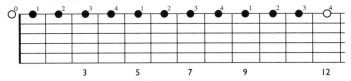

Below is a three-octave chromatic scale starting on the open low-E string. Once again, strive for a nice even sound.

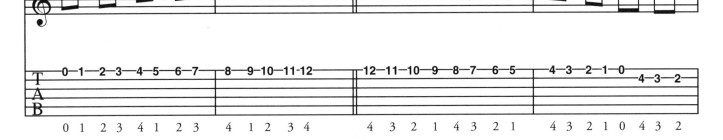

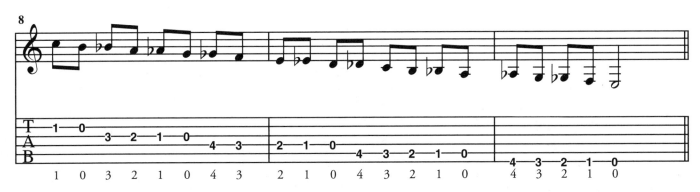

Chapter 3: The Major Scale

Major Scale Construction

Most of our musical resources are derived from the *major scale*. A major scale can begin on any one of the 12 tones found in the chromatic scale (page 10); this starting tone is called the *tonic*, or root, and gives the scale its name. Scales are usually constructed from formulas that we apply to the chromatic scale. Let's see how this works. The formula for the major scale is: Whole Step–Whole Step–Half Step–Whole Step–Whole Step–Whole Step–Half Step.

Each tone in the scale can be labelled with a number called a *scale degree*. These numbers will be very useful as we delve deeper into jazz theory.

Below is a two-octave chromatic scale beginning on A.

If we apply the major scale formula, beginning on C, we'll end up with a C Major scale.

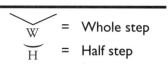

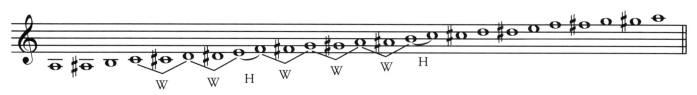

C Major Scale

Here is the same idea beginning on G. The result is a G Major scale.

G Major Scale

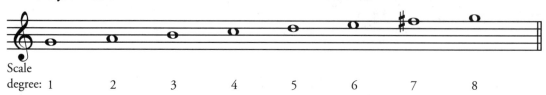

Since there are 12 possible starting notes in the chromatic scale, we can see that there are fundamentally 12 major scales or major keys. A *key* consists of all the notes of a particular scale. A song or tune is said to be *in* a particular key if its melody and accompaniment are based on the corresponding major scale. For example, a song whose melody and accompaniment are based on the G Major scale is said to be in the key of G Major or just the "key of G." Of course, jazz tunes contain many chords and notes that lie outside of the key, but you should always keep the song's key in mind as the "home base" to which you will return.

At this point it would be an excellent idea to construct all 12 scales on paper. After doing so, you will realize that each scale (or key) has a different number of sharps or flats. The major scales F, B♭, E♭, A♭, D♭ and G♭ utilize flat signs, while B, E, A, D and G use sharp signs instead. The C Major scale contains no sharps or flats.

It is important to realize that notes that are *enharmonic equivalents* (same pitch, different note names) also produce equivalent major scales and keys. In other words, the actual pitches in both scales would be the same, but they would be notated differently. Including the scales that are enharmonic equivalents increases the number of major scales to 15. For example, an F♯ Major scale contains the same pitches as a G♭ Major scale, but they would be notated like this:

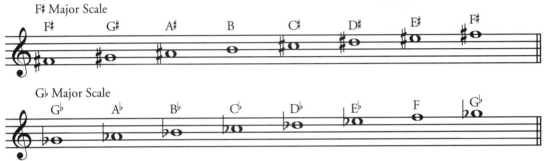

In most jazz music, the keys of C♯, C♭ and F♯ are rarely seen. So, we generally think in terms of there being 12 major scales representing 12 different keys. They are:

C, F, B♭, E♭, A♭, D♭, G♭, B, E, A, D, G.

The Circle of 4ths/5ths

You may be wondering why the keys and scales are listed in this order. Over many centuries, an important tool has emerged. This tool is called the *circle* (or *cycle*) *of 4ths* or the *circle of 5ths*. You will see this circle over and over again throughout your study of jazz, or any other kind of music, for that matter. How you use it depends on what you are studying, as it has many applications. Right now let's just take a look at its basic layout:

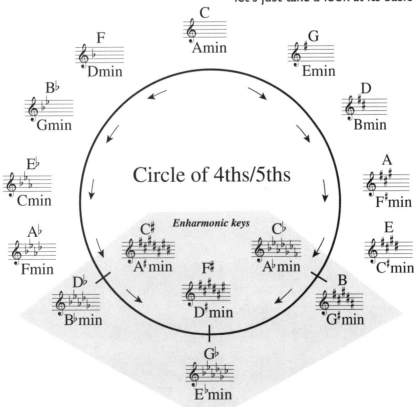

As you can see, all 12 major keys (or scales) surround the circle. If you move *counter-clockwise*, each key or scale is exactly four major scale degrees higher than the previous key or scale. (For example, moving C–D–E–F, we see F is a 4th above C.) When looked at from this perspective, this tool is called the circle of 4ths. If you move *clockwise* through the circle, each note is five major scale degrees above the previous note (C–D–E–F–G; G is a 5th above C), which is why this tool can be called the circle of 5ths as well. In most jazz studies, we tend to use the term circle of 4ths.

At the moment, we are using the circle simply to organize the 12 scales or keys. Why is this necessary? It is necessary because it is very important to memorize all the notes in each major scale and learning the scales in this order makes this job much easier. This is how:

The C Major scale has no sharps or flats—it's pretty easy to memorize. The major scales F through G♭ each have one more flat than the scale before it. In other words, F has one flat, B♭ has two, E♭ has three and so on until you reach G♭, which has six flats.

These scales are shown below. Notice that the fourth note in every scale is the "newly flatted" note, which is also the name of the next scale.

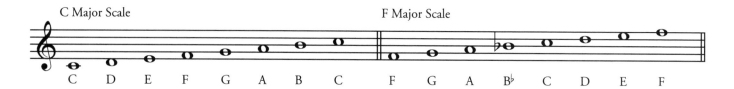

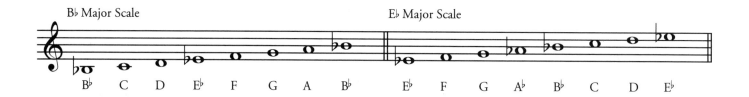

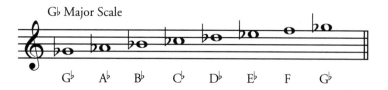

The major scales B through G each lose a sharp as you travel counter-clockwise through the circle. So B has five sharps, E has four sharps and so on until you reach G, which has only one sharp. The fourth note in the G Major scale is C, which of course brings you back to the beginning of the circle. The fourth note in each of these scales will be the "newly dropped" sharp and the name of the next scale. These scales are shown below.

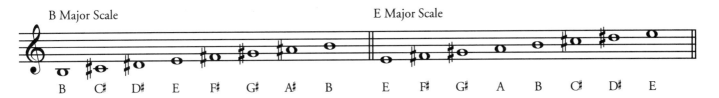

B Major Scale: B C# D# E F# G# A# B

E Major Scale: E F# G# A B C# D# E

A Major Scale: A B C# D E F# G# A

D Major Scale: D E F# G A B C# D

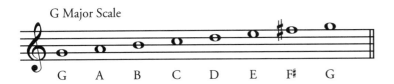

G Major Scale: G A B C D E F# G

When you look at the beginning of a piece of music, you will usually find what we call the *key signature*. This is the area between the treble clef and the time signature. If you see a single flat sign, the song is in the key of F, because the F scale contains only one flat. Two flats would mean the song is in B♭, because the B♭ scale contains two flats, and so on.

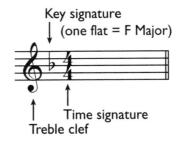

Key signature
(one flat = F Major)

Treble clef

Time signature

Below are all of the major key signatures.

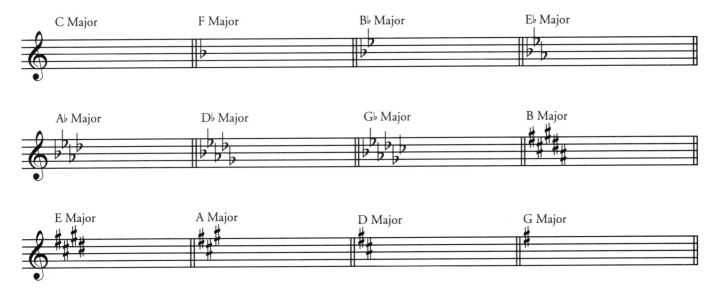

C Major   F Major   B♭ Major   E♭ Major

A♭ Major   D♭ Major   G♭ Major   B Major

E Major   A Major   D Major   G Major

Now, stop and memorize all the major scales in circle of 4ths order. You will be rewarded for this over and over again as you learn more about jazz and music in general. Memorize what each key signature looks like as well.

Horizontal Major Scale Fingerings

Now, let's play these major scales on the fretboard. We'll explore three different ways of doing this. We'll start with horizontal fingerings, move on to one-octave vertical fingerings and finally, two-octave vertical fingerings.

Horizontal fingerings are those that travel along a single string. We start with these because it's easy to see the scale's formula laid out this way. The following example shows six horizontal fingerings, one on each string. Study these examples, then try to work out all 12 major scales on each string. Doing this will help you learn the names of the notes all over the fretboard, especially if you're still a little fuzzy in this regard.

◼ = *Downstroke*—Downward motion of your pick.

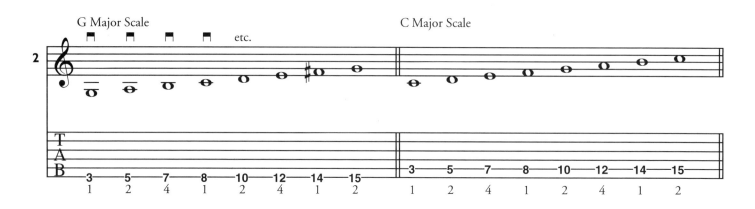

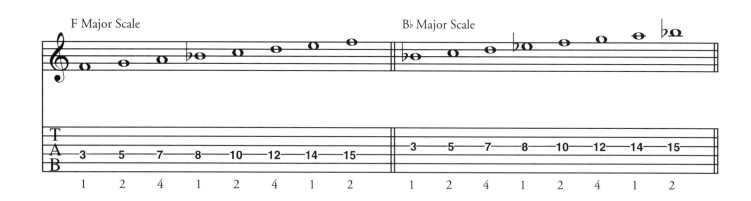

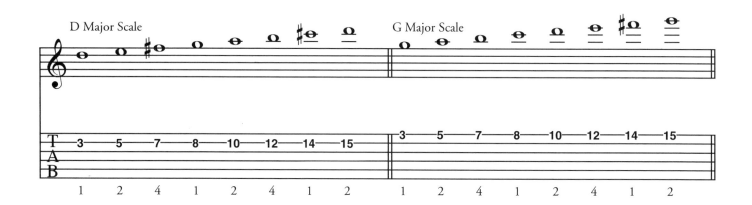

One-Octave Vertical Fingerings

Vertical fingerings are those that use more than one string, allowing your hand to stay in the same position. Following are five different vertical major scale fingerings. These should be memorized and practiced so you can play each fingering in all 12 keys. Pay strict attention to your sound. Every note should be equal in terms of volume and tone.

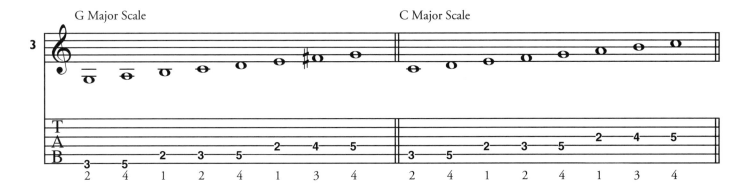

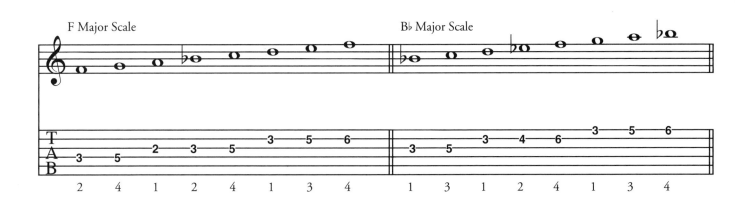

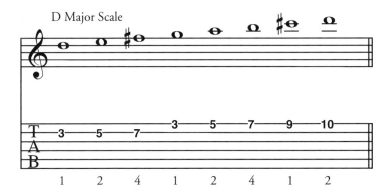

Two-Octave Vertical Fingerings

These fingerings cover two octaves and all six strings. The notes in parentheses are notes that lie above and below the lowest and highest tonics (or roots) in the scale. First, practice the scales from root to root. When the scales are learned in this form, start adding the additional notes so you learn to see them as a part of the scale.

There are six different fingerings in this system: three whose roots are found on the 6th string and three with roots on the 5th string.

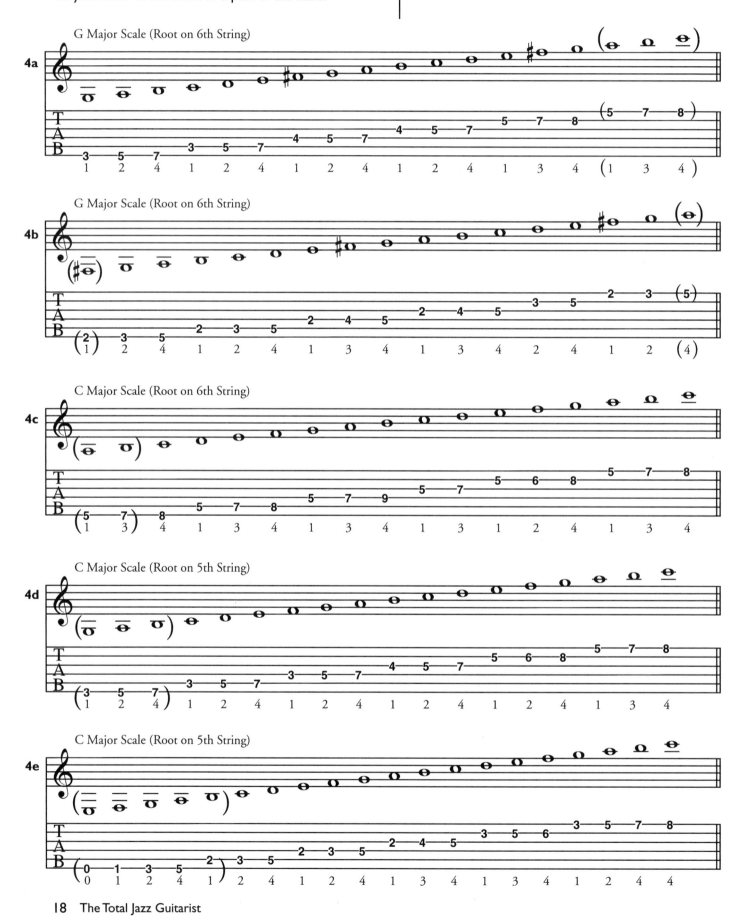

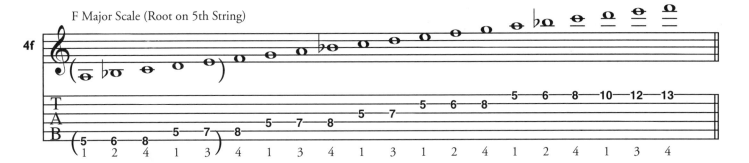

F Major Scale (Root on 5th String)

Learning and Practicing the Major Scales

Rather than trying to learn an entire fingering at one time, you might want to learn the fingering on two strings at a time.

First practice the notes of a scale on only the 6th and 5th strings. Practice the pattern over and over until it feels comfortable. Then, practice the notes on only the 5th and 4th strings. When this is comfortable, the patterns on the 6th, 5th and 4th strings should be combined and practiced. Then work on the 4th and 3rd strings, later adding the 2nd and 1st strings. Working on scales in this way is very efficient and helps to make the new fingerings seem much less overwhelming. It's also a great way to find new melodic possibilities.

Students who practice scales for years and years actually waste a lot of time. Once a scale fingering is learned, it is a better idea to practice *using* the scale in an improvisational context. Much more will be said about this later, but for now we need to look at ways to practice these scales while you're first learning them. The following method has worked for many jazz guitar students.

1. **Practice the scales *chromatically*, or a half step apart.** Just start the scale on the lowest note possible. Play the scale ascending and descending. Then, move up one fret and do it again. Cover the entire fretboard this way. You may find the scales easier to play if you alternate between downstrokes and upstrokes of the pick.

∨ = *Upstroke*—Upward motion of your pick.

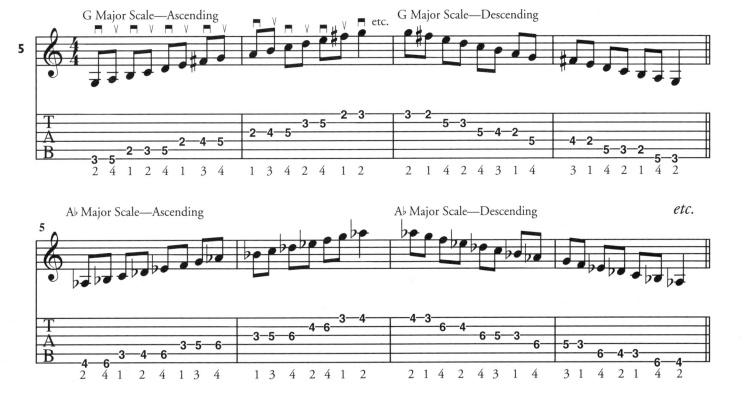

2. **Practice the scales a whole step apart.** Start the scale on the lowest note possible. Play the scale ascending and descending. Then move up two frets and repeat. Once again, cover the entire fretboard.

3. **Practice the scales a *minor third* (three half steps) apart.** Start the scale on the lowest note possible. Play the scale ascending and descending. Then move up three frets and repeat. Once again, cover the entire fretboard.

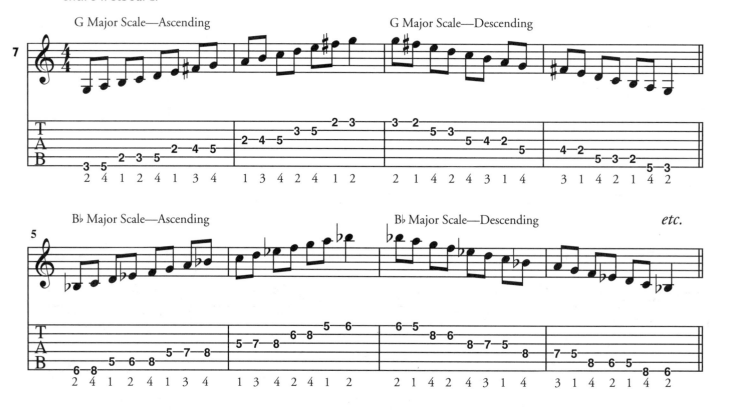

4. **Practice the scales a *fourth* (five half steps) apart.** Start with a C tonic. Then move to an F tonic, followed by B♭, E♭, A♭, D♭, G♭, B, E, A, D and finally G. This is simply moving counter-clockwise around the circle of 4ths.

5. **Practice the scales a *fifth* (seven half steps) apart.** Start with G and move on to D, A, E, B, G♭, D♭, A♭, E♭, B♭, F and finally C. This, of course, is moving clockwise around the circle of 5ths.

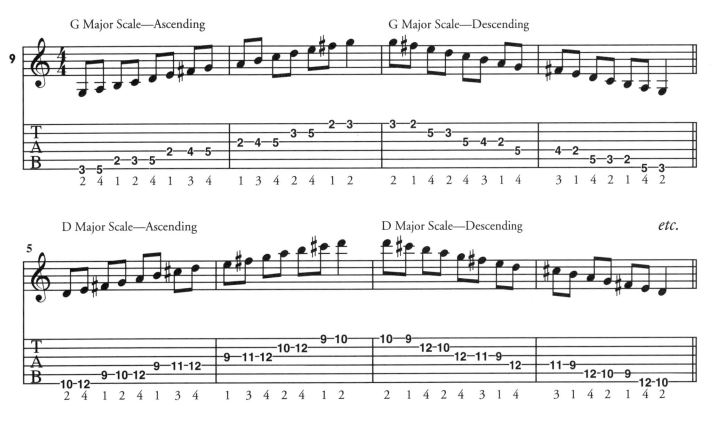

6. All of the above ideas can be practiced another way as well: alternating ascending and descending scales. In other words, if you are practicing chromatically, you would first play the ascending scale, then move up to the next fret and play the descending scale. Move up again and ascend. Move up again and descend, and proceed up and down the fretboard in this manner. The same approach can be used with whole steps, minor 3rds, 4ths and 5ths as well.

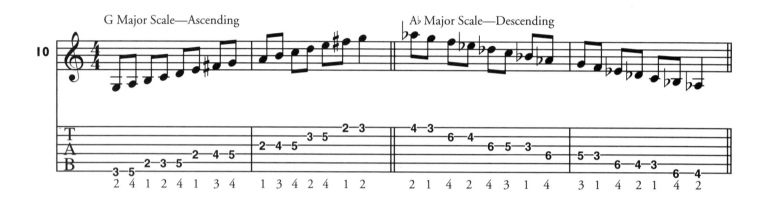

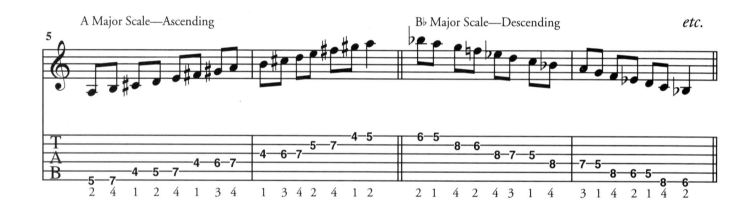

Chapter 4: Melodic Patterns

Melodic patterns, or *sequences,* are a good way to develop your hands and will give you many melodic ideas to use in improvised solos. The idea is to take a short melodic idea and move it up or down to start on different notes of the scale. For example, if you start with the melodic idea 1–2–3, a melodic pattern would be 1–2–3, 2–3–4, 3–4–5, etc. You should strive to learn a lot of these.

Below are six common melodic patterns. You should practice them using all six major scale fingerings shown previously (pages 18–19) and transpose them to all keys. You may find these tricky at first. Just be patient, learn one at a time, and practice slowly. You'll eventually find them becoming easier and easier.

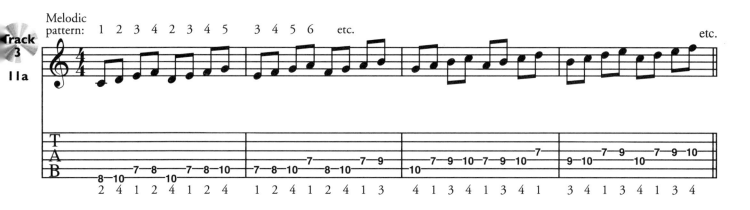

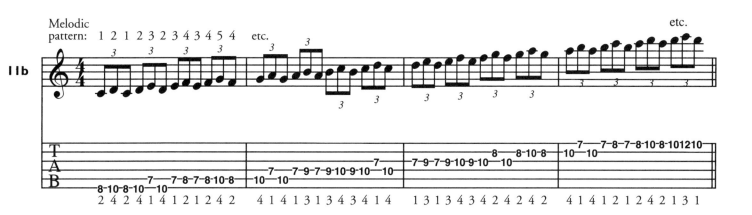

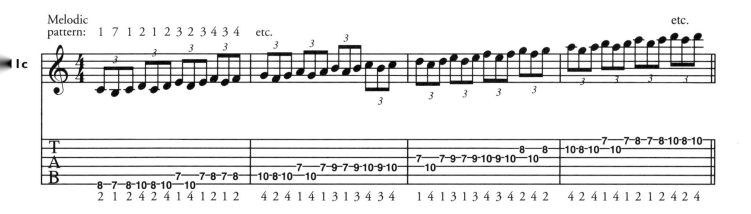

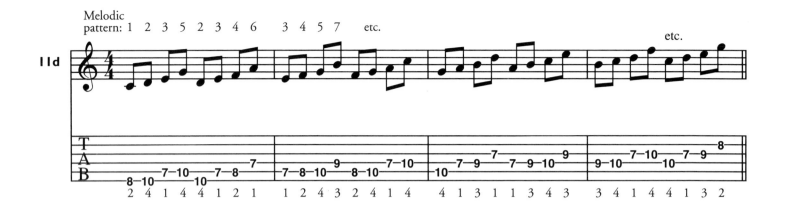

Melodic pattern: 1 2 3 5 2 3 4 6   3 4 5 7   etc.

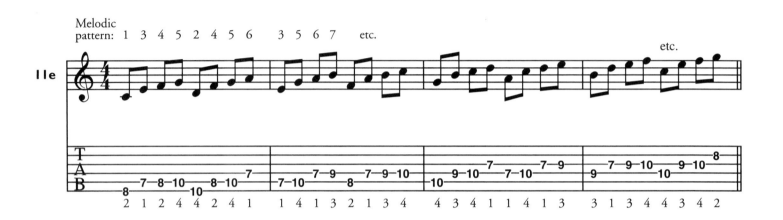

Melodic pattern: 1 3 4 5 2 4 5 6   3 5 6 7   etc.

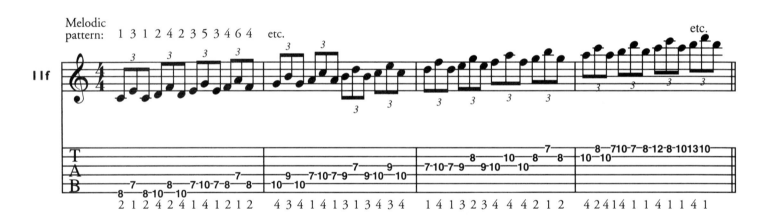

Melodic pattern: 1 3 1 2 4 2 3 5 3 4 6 4   etc.

Creating Your Own Melodic Patterns

Here is a fun and simple way to create your own melodic patterns or sequences.

1. Write out a two octave scale (you can use any kind of scale of course; this example uses an A Minor Pentatonic scale).

A Minor Pentatonic Scale

2. Number each note in the scale.

1   2   3   4   5   6   7   8   9   10   11   12

3. Choose four numbers at random.

1–3–4–2

4. Sequence the numbers. In other words, starting a new row, increase each number by one. Continue this process until several rows have been created.

1–3–4–2
2–4–5–3
3–5–6–4
4–6–7–5
5–7–8–6
6–8–9–7
7–9–10–8
8–10–11–9

5. Translate the numbers back into notes and practice, practice, practice.

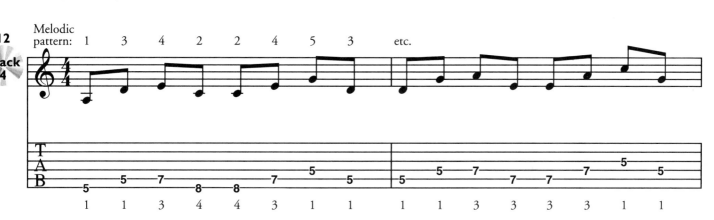

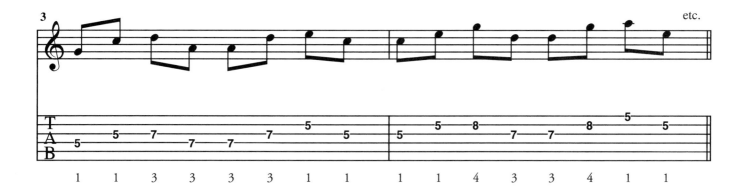

Chapter 5: Triads

Triads are the three-note chords upon which most other chords are built. Like so many other areas in music, triads are based on formulas that we plug into major scales. For our purposes here, there are four different kinds of triads: major, minor, diminished and augmented. Let's take a look at each one.

Major Triads

To build a *major triad*, we combine the tonic or root (R), the 3rd and the 5th notes of any major scale, hence the formula: R–3–5. The following example shows this formula applied to a C Major scale. Combining the notes C, E and G produces a C Major triad.

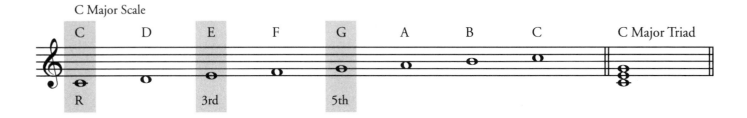

Here is another example based on a G Major scale.

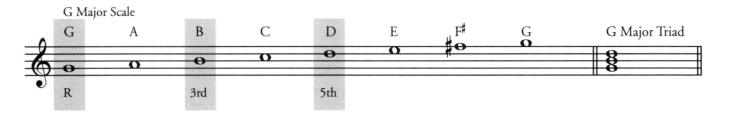

It's really not very complicated, but there is a little more to know. By choosing different *voicings*, we can place these notes in different orders and the name of the triad remains the same—and we have a systematic way of doing this.

Below is a C Major triad. The notes from bottom to top are C–E–G. When the notes are sounded in this order, the triad is in *root position*.

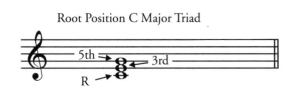

Root Position C Major Triad

We *invert* a triad when we take the bottom note and place it one octave higher. This triad is now sounded E–G–C and is still a C Major triad, but now we say that it is in the *1st inversion*.

Now, we can do this one more time. Raising the E one octave will give us G–C–E. We would now say that this C Major triad is in the *2nd inversion*.

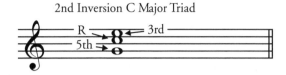

Now would be a great time for you to write out all 12 major triads in root position, 1st inversion and 2nd inversion. If you have memorized your major scales, this shouldn't take you too long.

Minor Triads

The formula for a *minor triad* is: R–♭3–5. In other words, we start with the root of the major scale, add the lowered 3rd, add the 5th and voilà, we have constructed a minor triad. Here are two examples based on the F and B♭ Major scales.

You can invert minor triads, too.

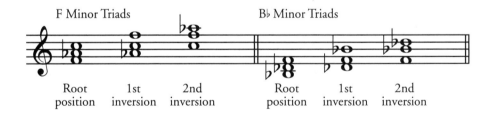

Now, practice writing out all of the minor triads in each inversion.

Diminished Triads

The formula for a *diminished triad* is: R–♭3–♭5. Start with the root of any major scale, add the lowered 3rd and the lowered 5th, and you get a diminished triad, abbreviated with the chord symbol dim, as in Cdim. Here are two examples based on the C and G Major scales.

Once again, you can invert diminished triads in the same way.

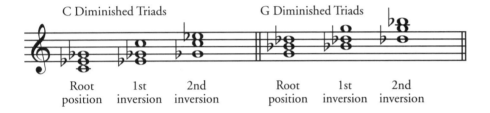

| Root position | 1st inversion | 2nd inversion | | Root position | 1st inversion | 2nd inversion |

Now, write out all 12 diminished triads and their inversions.

Augmented Triads

The formula for an *augmented triad* is: R–3–♯5. Just combine the root, the 3rd and the raised 5th of any major scale and you have an augmented triad. The chord symbol used in this book is aug; you may also see +. The examples below are based on the D and G Major scales.

Of course, you can invert these as well.

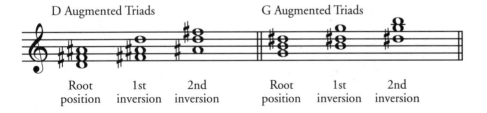

| Root position | 1st inversion | 2nd inversion | | Root position | 1st inversion | 2nd inversion |

Again, write out all 12 augmented triads and their inversions.

Finding Triads on the Fretboard

In this system, we divide the guitar into four *string sets* consisting of three strings each.

- Strings 6–5–4 form the 1st string set.
- Strings 5–4–3 form the 2nd string set.
- Strings 4–3–2 form the 3rd string set.
- Strings 3–2–1 form the 4th string set.

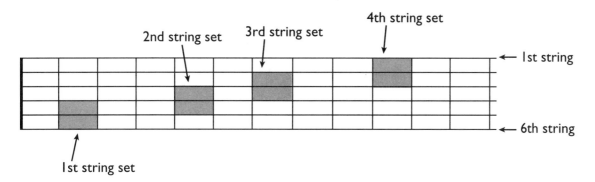

Your job is to find and memorize all the major, minor, diminished and augmented triads, in all keys and inversions on all four string sets. Let's begin with a root position C Major triad on the 1st string set.

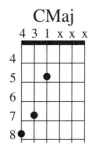

Now that you know the shape of this movable root position C Major triad on the 1st string set, you know the remaining 11 triads as well. By playing this same shape rooted at the 13th fret we get an F Major triad. At the 6th fret it becomes a B♭ Major triad and so on.

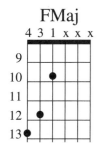
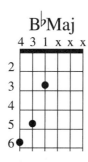

Now, let's take our root position C Major triad and turn it into a minor triad. Lower E, the 3rd, to E♭. Then, practice this minor triad shape from each root, going around the circle of 4ths.

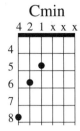

To the right is the root position diminished triad shape. Practice this shape in the same way as the major triad shape.

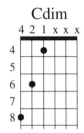

Finally, we come to the augmented shape.

Work with all of these shapes in all keys.

Following are the root position triad shapes on the remaining three string sets. Practice them in exactly the same way as you worked with the previous examples.

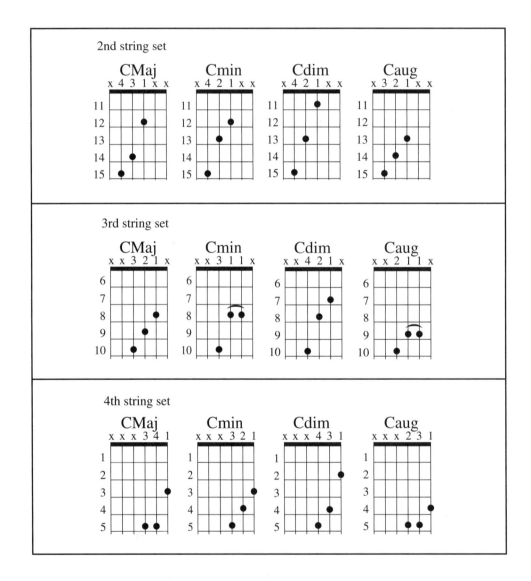

1st Inversion Triads

We can learn all the 1st inversion triads the same way. The following example shows major, minor, diminished and augmented 1st inversion triads on all the string sets. Be sure to learn these well before moving on to the 2nd inversion triads.

Most students find these a little trickier to memorize. Just remember that the root is the highest pitched note in the chord and let that guide you around the fretboard.

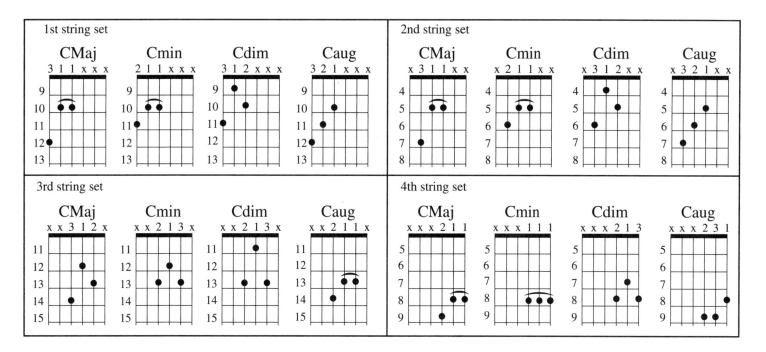

2nd Inversion Triads

Here they are—you know the drill. Work with the 2nd inversion triads below until you can play them in any order, in any key and on any string set. Remembering that the root is the middle tone in each triad will help you find your way around the fretboard with these shapes.

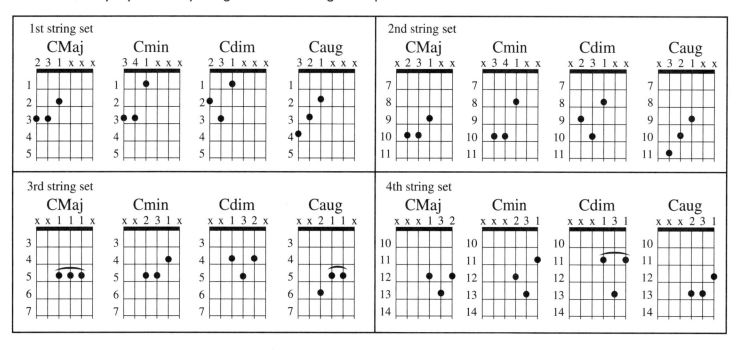

A few things to remember to make this job easier:

1. Triad shapes on the first two string sets will always be identical.
2. For now, finger these shapes any way that's comfortable. This exercise is more about note identification than coming up with great sounding, playable chords.
3. Augmented shapes remain the same on each string set, regardless of inversion.
4. Recite the note names in each triad as you practice them. This will burn the info into your mind.

Why Am I Doing This?

The amount of fretboard knowledge you derive from exploring triads in this way is nothing short of amazing. You will learn note location, discover new patterns and memorize pitch relationships. Later on, you will be able to construct larger chords using these triads as a starting point. As we begin discussing improvisational techniques, you will find yourself coming back to these triads over and over again.

Chapter 6: Major Family Chords

If you are comfortable with all the triads from the last chapter, it's time to turn your attention to larger chords. In this section, you'll be learning about *6th chords, 7th chords* and *extended chords*. Most jazz musicians think in terms of there being three broad families of chords—major, minor and dominant. There are also diminished and half diminished chords which can be thought of as existing within their own little category.

We'll be taking a look at all these different chords, learning about their construction, and becoming familiar with several sample voicings of each. Remember that learning about jazz harmony can be a lifetime study, and you'll always want (and need) new chord shapes. In the second section of this book, you will learn many more chords while working through actual tunes.

Major 6th Chords

Major chords are constructed from major triads. The simplest major chord beyond the triad is the *major sixth* chord. The formula for this type of chord is: R–3–5–6. Because the first three notes are just a major triad, you can think of this chord as a major triad with an added 6th. A major 6th chord is often abbreviated using a *chord symbol,* usually the root name and the number 6, as in F6, B♭6 and so on.

Applying the major 6th formula (R–3–5–6) to a C Major scale produces a C6 chord (see below).

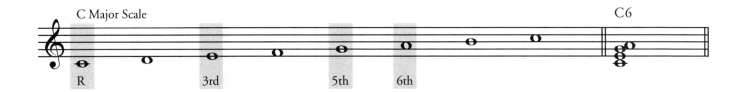

Below are four common voicings for major 6th chords. Learn them, and then practice playing them from all 12 roots.

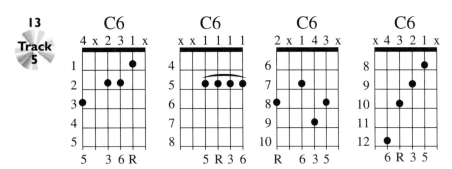

Major 7th Chords

The formula for a *major 7th* chord is: R–3–5–7. You will see major 7th chords designated in the following ways: CMaj7, CM7, Cma7 and C△7. For consistency, we will use Maj7 throughout this book. On paper, a CMaj7 chord would look like this:

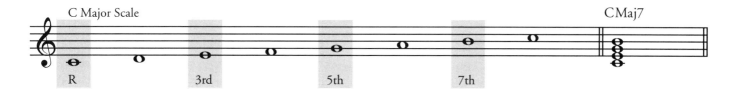

Here are four common ways to play this chord:

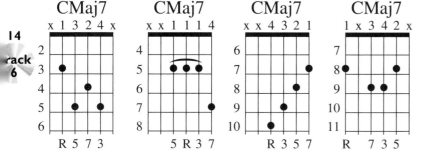

A Cool Way to Learn New Chords

Major 6th and major 7th chords each contain four notes. Since both of these chords start with major triads, and since you've just spent a lot of time learning triad shapes all over the fretboard, it seems reasonable that you can combine this information to build quite a few of these four note chords.

Here's how it works. You have learned major triads in root position, 1st inversion and 2nd inversion on four different string sets. This gives you 12 possible starting points to construct any four note major chord. Let's build some major 6th chords from these 12 starting points and see what we come up with. The examples below are based on the major triads of the 4th string set. Be sure you can "see" the triad in each chord shape. For the following examples, the dot for the added 6th is gray.

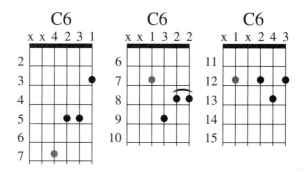

Here are some ideas based on triads of the 3rd string set:

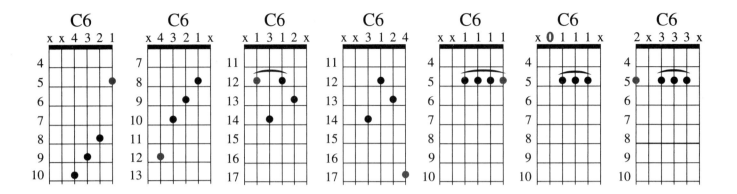

Now for the 2nd string set:

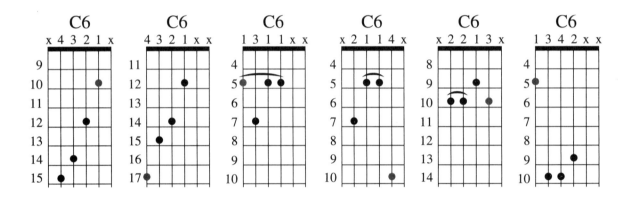

And finally, the 1st string set:

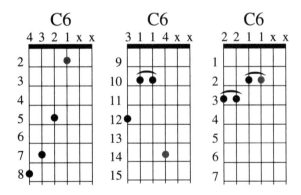

So, you can see that this system produces quite a few possibilities. Not every chord is usable in every musical context, but the idea is to see what is available on the fretboard. Don't feel like you have to know every single voicing shown here. Just memorize, transpose and use the ones you like. Later, if you feel the need for a bigger chord vocabulary, you'll know where to get a few more voicings.

Extended Chords

The term *extended chords* refers to chords that include notes that lie beyond a one-octave major scale. The common tones we add to chords are the 9th, 11th and 13th.

Extended chords and altered chords (see page 52) have a lot to do with making jazz sound like jazz. The late, great guitarist Ted Greene was fond of saying that "jazz lives above the 7th." There is much truth to that statement.

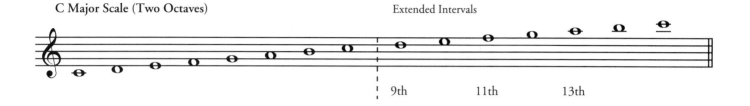

Major add 9th Chords

Major add 9th chords are four-note chords. The formula is: R–3–5–9 and the usual chord symbol is add9.

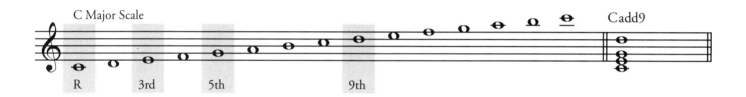

Here are a few voicings:

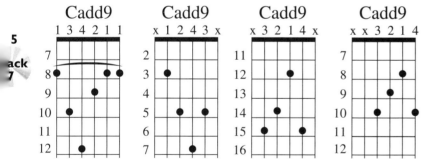

Major 9th Chords

Major 9th chords differ from major add 9th chords in that their formula includes the seventh: R–3–5–7–9. The following chord symbols designate major 9th chords: Maj9 and M9. This book will use the Maj9 chord symbol. On paper, a CMaj9 chord looks like this:

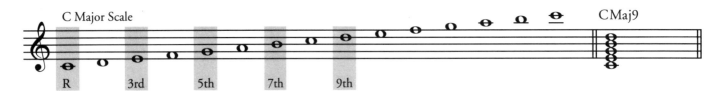

You may learn some voicings of this chord that do not contain all of these notes. You should know that it is common to omit certain notes in any chord. You'll find guidelines for this on page 42.

Here are some Maj9 chord shapes:

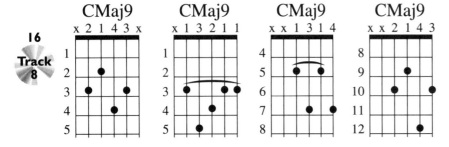

Major 13th Chords

The formula for a *major 13th chord* is: R–3–5–7–9–13. It is designated with the chord symbol Maj13. On paper, the chord looks like this:

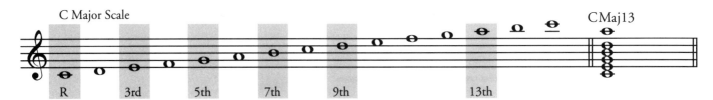

Some common voicings:

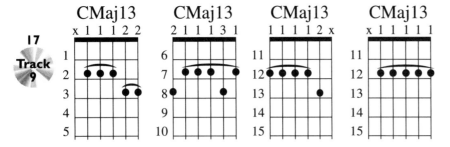

Note: You may be wondering why we have not included the *major 11th chord*. The 11th of the major scale is the same note as the 4th, but one octave higher. In a C scale, we're talking about the note F. Including this note in a major type chord would create a clash with the 3rd of the chord, which would be E. There aren't too many occasions where one would choose to utilize this unpleasant sound. There are times when we do include a raised or sharp 11th. Raising the F to an F♯ creates enough of an intervallic distance from E (the 3rd of the chord) to make the resulting harmony much more desirable.

Chapter 7: Minor Family Chords

Minor 6th Chords

Minor chords are constructed from minor triads. The simplest minor chord beyond the triad is the *minor 6th chord*. The formula for this type of chord is: R–♭3–5–6. You can see that the first three notes are a minor triad, so you can think of this chord as a minor triad with an added 6th.

Applying this formula to a C Minor scale produces a C Minor 6th chord.

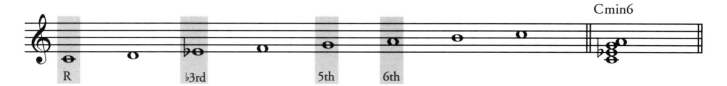

The chord symbol for minor 6th chords is usually the root name and min6, as in Fmin6, B♭min6 and so on.

Below are four common voicings for minor 6th chords. Learn them, and then practice playing them from all 12 roots.

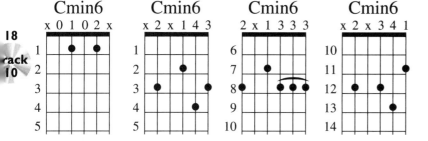

Minor Add 9th Chords

Minor add 9th chords are four-note chords. The formula is: R–♭3–5–9, and the usual chord symbol is Cmin add9.

Some voicings:

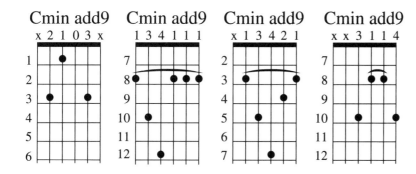

Minor 7th Chords

The formula for a *minor 7th chord* is: R–♭3–5–♭7. You will see minor 7th chords designated in the following ways: Cm7, Cmin7, Cmi7 and C-7. This book uses the Cmin7 symbol. On paper, a Cmin7 chord would look like this:

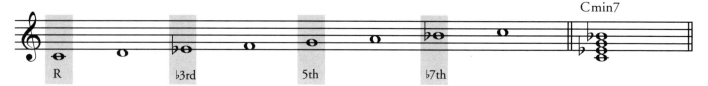

Here are four common ways to play this chord:

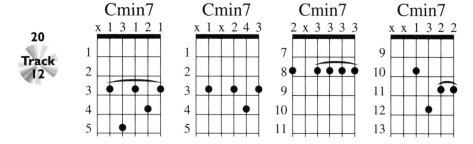

Minor 9th Chords

Minor 9th chords differ from minor add9 chords in that their formula includes the ♭7th: R–♭3–5–♭7–9. The following chord symbols designate minor 9th chords: m9, min9 and possibly -9. We will use min9 for this book. On paper, a Cmin9 chord looks like this:

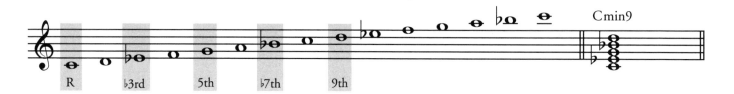

Here are some min9 chord shapes:

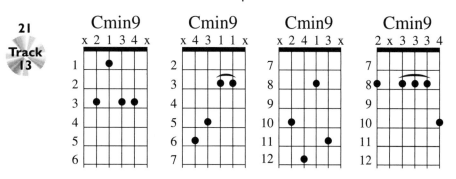

Minor 11th Chords

The formula for a *minor 11th chord* is: R–♭3–5–♭7–9–11. The following chord symbols designate minor 11th chords: m11, min11 and possibly -11. We will use min11 in this book. On paper, the chord looks like this:

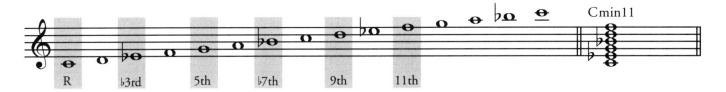

Some voicings:

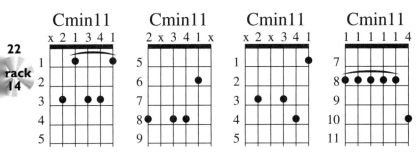

Note: Minor 11th chords are commonly used even though major 11th chords are not. The reason is that the ♭3 and 11 (the 4 in the higher octave) are a whole step apart and do not clash with each other (see note on page 36).

Minor 13th Chords

The formula for a *minor 13th chord* is: R–♭3–5–♭7–9–13. They are designated with the chord symbol min13 (which we'll use in this book), m13 or -13. On paper, the chord looks like this:

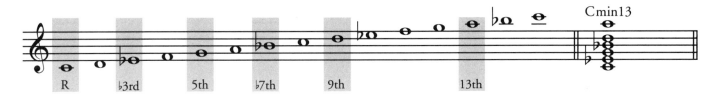

Some common voicings:

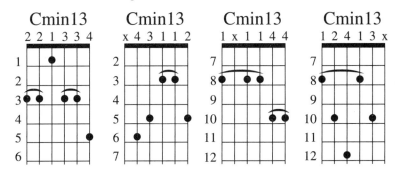

Chapter 8: Dominant Family Chords

Dominant 7th Chords

The formula for a *dominant 7th chord* is: R–3–5–♭7.
Dominant 7th chords are designated in this way: C7.
On paper, a C7 chord would look like this:

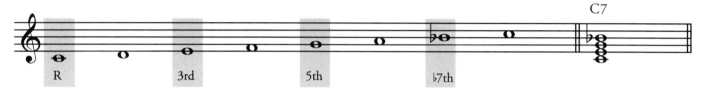

Here are four common ways to play this chord:

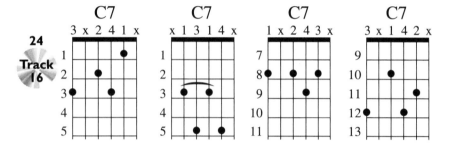

Dominant 9th Chords

The formula for a *dominant 9th chord* is: R–3–5–♭7–9.
Dominant 9th chords are designated like this: C9.

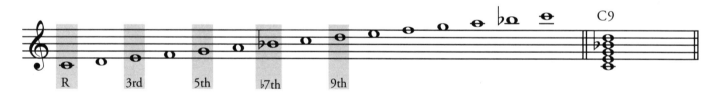

Here are some dominant 9th chord shapes:

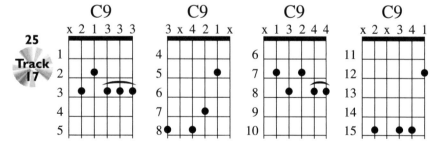

Dominant 11th Chords

The formula for a *dominant 11th chord* is: R–3–5–♭7–9–11.
They are designated like this: C11. On paper, the chord
looks like this:

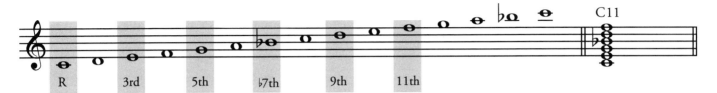

Some voicings:

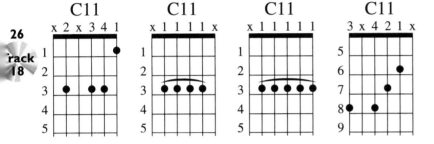

Dominant 13th Chords

The formula for a *dominant 13th chord* is: R–3–5–♭7–9–13.
They are written like this: C13. On paper, the chord looks
like this:

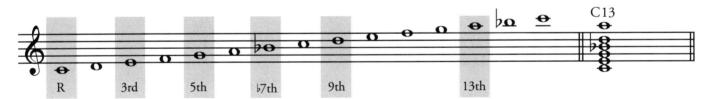

Some common voicings:

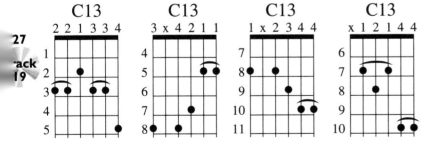

Chapter 9: Half-Diminished 7th and Full-Diminished 7th Chords

Even though *diminished 7th* and *half-diminished 7th chords* do not fall neatly into the major, minor or dominant families, they are essential to jazz.

The formula for a half-diminished 7th chord is: R–♭3–♭5–♭7. They are written like this: C⌀7, Cmin7♭5 or Cm7♭5. In this book, we'll use Cmin7♭5. On paper, they look like this:

Here are a few fingerings:

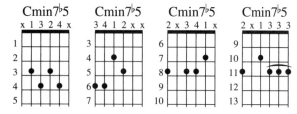

The formula for a *full-diminished 7th chord* is: R–♭3–♭5–♭♭7 and it is written like this: C°7 or Cdim7. This book uses the Cdim7 chord symbol. The *double-flatted 7th* (♭♭7) is enharmonically equivalent to the 6th degree of a major scale.

Sometimes when you are learning a new tune, you may see a full-diminished 7th chord written like this: R–♭3–♭5–6. In this book, we will use the ♭♭7 notation because it more accurately describes the function of the chord.

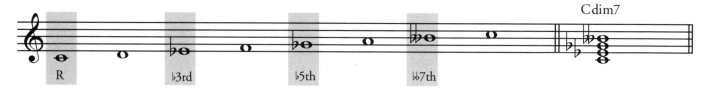

Here are a few fingerings:

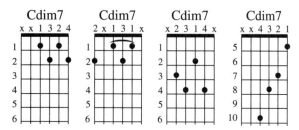

Omitting Chord Tones

Because the guitar has only six strings and you have only four fingers to work with, it is common to omit certain notes when playing many of the chords we have discussed. Keep in mind:

- You can drop the root if you keep the 5th and vice versa.
- 9ths are sometimes eliminated when playing 11th and 13th chords.
- 3rds and 7ths are rarely omitted because they determine whether a chord is major, minor or dominant.

Also, remember that these sample fingerings are only the beginning. You will probably be investigating new fingerings for as long as you play the guitar.

Chapter 10: Diatonic Harmony

Harmonized Major Scales

After students learn how to construct the various kinds of chords and fingerings, they often wonder how to keep track of them all. One way is to organize them by keys, a process called *diatonic harmony*. We can find out which chords belong to a key by simply *stacking 3rds* above each tone in a major scale. Below, we have a C Major scale where each tone has been harmonized with 3rds. (You can also think of 3rds as simply every other note in the scale.) When we do this, we produce seven different chords. These are the chords that are *diatonic*, or natural, to the scale. They were all created with notes from the same scale and therefore "belong" together.

Harmonized C Major Scale

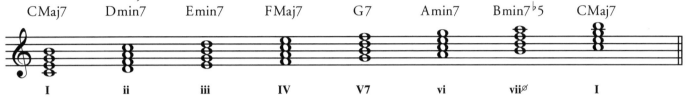

All major scales have the same structure and produce the same types of chords. The first (I) and fourth (IV) chords will always be major 7th chords. The second (ii), third (iii) and sixth (vi) chords will always be minor 7th chords. The fifth chord (V7) is always a dominant 7th, and the seventh chord (vii⌀) will be half-diminished. Because of this, musicians usually use Roman numerals as a sort of shorthand to organize all the chords in all the keys. This way, if you know the notes in all the major scales, then you also know all the diatonic chords as well. Upper case Roman numerals are used to designate major and dominant chords, while lower case numerals designate minor and half-diminished chords.

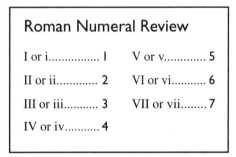

I Chords	+	IV Chords		=	Always Major 7th
ii Chords	+ iii Chords +	vi Chords		=	Always Minor 7th
		V7* Chords		=	Always Dominant 7th
		vii Chords		=	Always ⌀7th

* Here, the "7" signifies the dominant quality

Roman Numeral Review

I or i.............. I	V or v............ 5
II or ii............ 2	VI or vi........... 6
III or iii.......... 3	VII or vii........ 7
IV or iv.......... 4	

Here are two more harmonized major scales that illustrate this point.

Harmonized G Major Scale

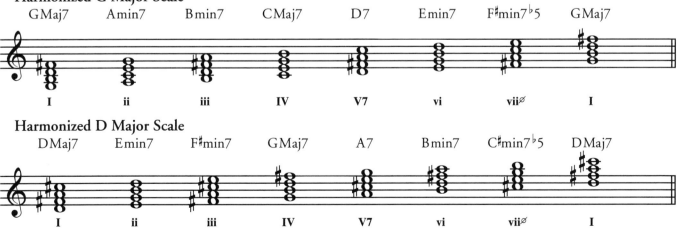

Harmonized D Major Scale

Building Harmonized Major Scales
on the Fretboard

To construct harmonized scales on the fretboard:

1. Start with any major 7th chord voicing.

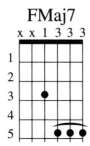

2. Move each note in the chord up to the next scale tone on the same string.

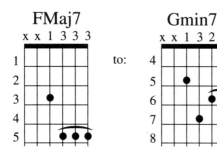

3. Continue this process until you arrive at the major 7th chord one octave higher than the chord with which you started.

Harmonized F Major Scale

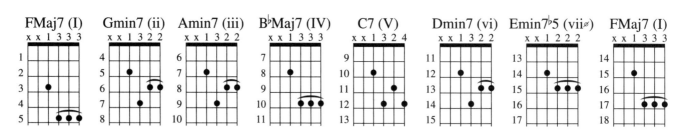

You should spend a lot of time and effort practicing this, working through all 12 keys, then starting over using a new major 7th chord voicing. Not only will you learn new chords this way, but you'll gain a much better understanding of how all the chords work together among all the keys. Below are several major 7th chords from which you should build harmonized scales.

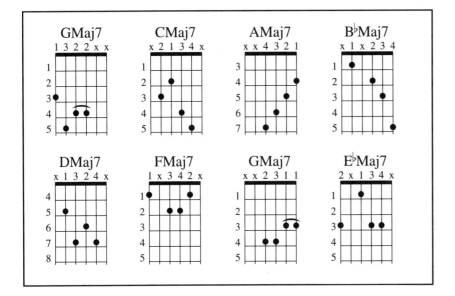

Diatonic Arpeggios of the Major Scale

After you are comfortable with the overall view of the major scale and its chord systems (referred to as diatonic harmony), it's usually a good idea to start working on *diatonic arpeggios*. Simply put, these are the chord tones that make up each chord in each key. You need to have a command of these over the entire range of the fretboard. Diatonic arpeggios will serve you well when you begin improvising solos over chord changes (page 100). There are quite a few systems for learning these arpeggios. The following system is based on the six major scale fingerings you learned earlier in this section.

The next examples show, first, a major scale fingering, then sample diatonic chord voicings along with arpeggio fingerings. It isn't necessary to learn *all* of this material before moving on. Learn and memorize one set of arpeggios, transposing the fingerings to all 12 keys. When you get hungry for more, you can always come back and pick up another set.

Diatonic Arpeggios of the Harmonized C Major Scale—Version 1

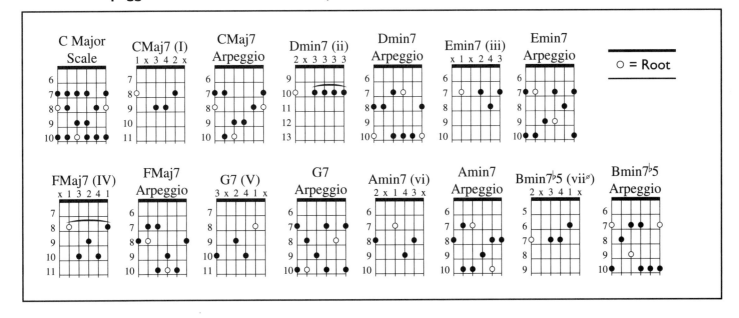

Diatonic Arpeggios of the Harmonized C Major Scale—Version 2

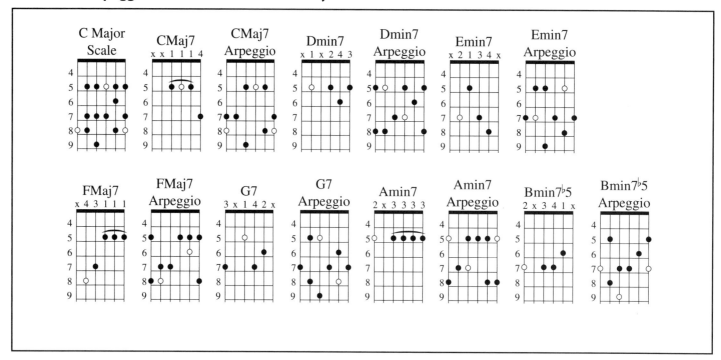

Diatonic Arpeggios of the Harmonized C Major Scale—Version 3

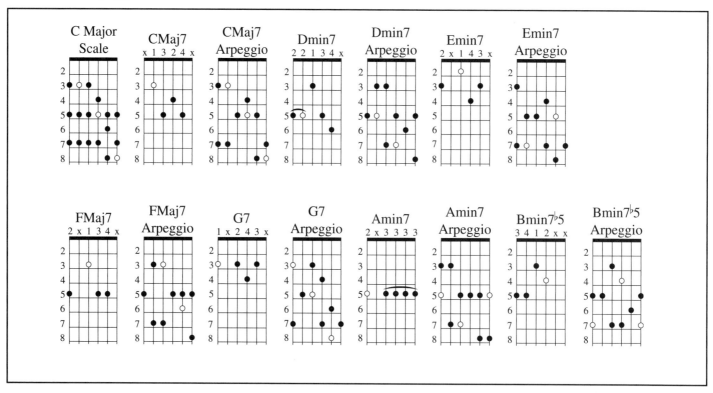

Diatonic Arpeggios of the Harmonized F Major Scale—Version 1

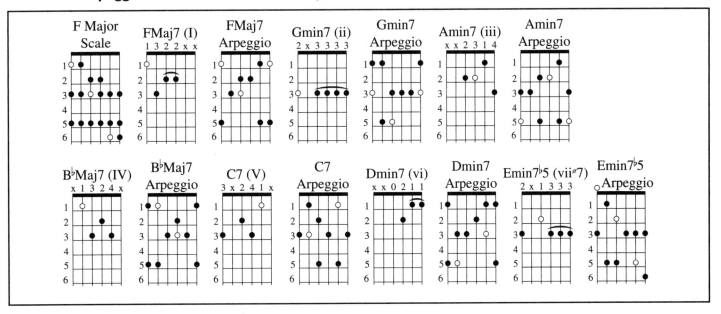

Diatonic Arpeggios of the Harmonized F Major Scale—Version 2

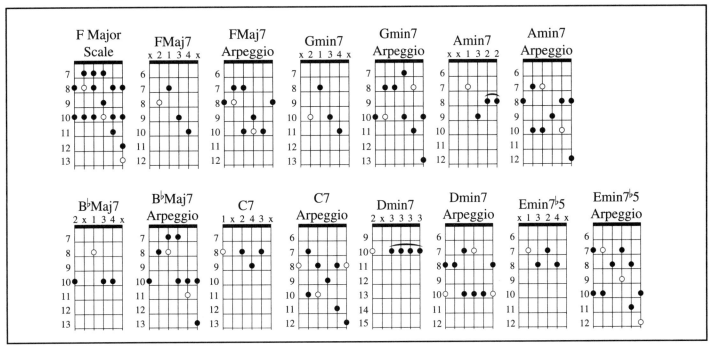

Diatonic Arpeggios of the Harmonized F Major Scale—Version 3

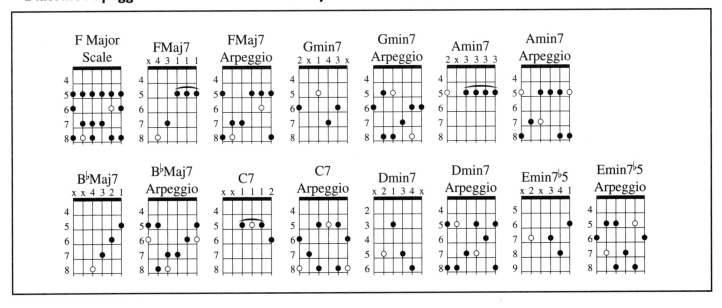

The Modes of the Major Scale

The next area of study that you should be familiar with is the concept of *modes*. Understanding the layout of *modal harmony* will help you understand the relationships between chords and scales a little better. While some jazz players think in terms of modes quite extensively, most others concentrate on other musical tools for improvisation. Still, understanding modes is an important area of study for all musicians.

You generate the modes of a scale by starting on any scale tone other than the root, and continuing through the scale until you arrive at the starting note again, one octave higher. In the example below, you can see that we've generated six new scales, or modes, from the C Major scale.

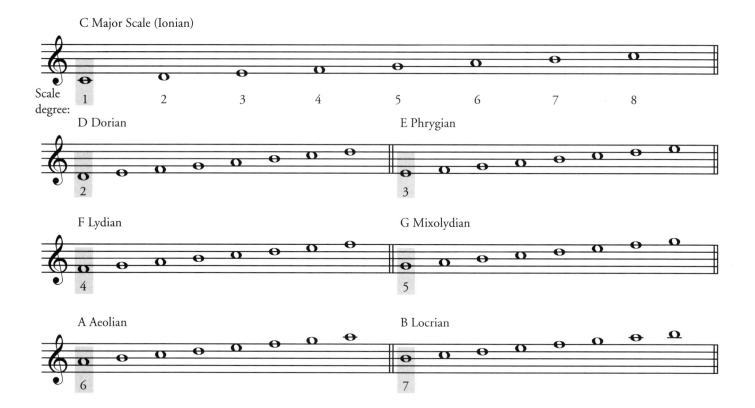

In the world of modes, the major scale is referred to as the *Ionian* mode. Starting on the note D and playing through the C scale until we reach D again produces a D *Dorian* mode. Going from E to E generates an E *Phrygian* mode. Going from F to F generates an F *Lydian* mode. Going from G to G generates a G *Mixolydian* mode. Going from A to A generates an A *Aeolian* mode. Going from B to B generates a B *Locrian* mode.

This pattern of modes is consistent across all major scales. Here is a list of the modes based on a G Major scale:

G to G = G Ionian

A to A = A Dorian

B to B = B Phrygian

C to C = C Lydian

D to D = D Mixolydian

E to E = E Aeolian

F♯ to F♯ = F♯ Locrian

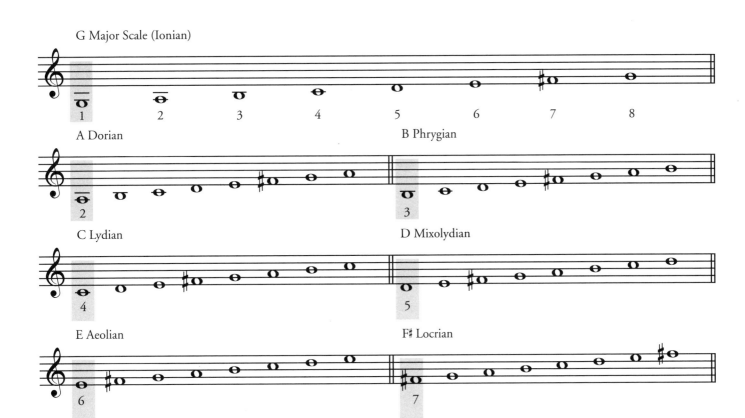

G Major Scale (Ionian)

A Dorian · B Phrygian

C Lydian · D Mixolydian

E Aeolian · F♯ Locrian

In Harmonized Major Scales (page 43), we discussed the chords that are part of each major scale. Now you will see that each chord in the scale corresponds to one of the modes. Another way to think about these chords is that each one is constructed with the root, 3rd, 5th and 7th of each mode.

C Ionian corresponds to CMaj7.

D Dorian corresponds to Dmin7.

E Phrygian corresponds to Emin7.

F Lydian corresponds to FMaj7.

G Mixolydian corresponds to G7.

A Aeolian corresponds to Amin7.

B Locrian corresponds to Bmin7♭5.

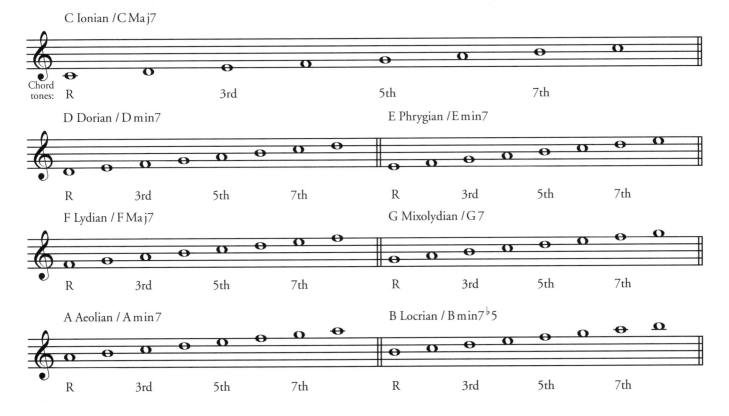

C Ionian / C Maj7

Chord tones: R · 3rd · 5th · 7th

D Dorian / D min7 · E Phrygian / E min7

R · 3rd · 5th · 7th · R · 3rd · 5th · 7th

F Lydian / F Maj7 · G Mixolydian / G 7

R · 3rd · 5th · 7th · R · 3rd · 5th · 7th

A Aeolian / A min7 · B Locrian / B min7♭5

R · 3rd · 5th · 7th · R · 3rd · 5th · 7th

What this means is that you can use a mode to improvise over its corresponding chord. In actuality, when you generate modes, you are creating new scales with which to improvise (or compose).

You should start memorizing the names of the modes and their corresponding chords in each key.

At this point, most students say something like, "Hey, wait a minute. All these modes are really just the C scale. Why can't I just think 'C scale' over all of these chords?" Well, you can, and many players do think this way while improvising over progressions that consist entirely of all or some of these diatonic chords.

The real value of the modes is that they can be used to improvise over chords that are *non-diatonic*, or not in the key. Look at the following progression:

(Jazz chord progressions are usually written using *slash notation*, where the chord name appears above a staff with one *slash* per beat. This means you can play the indicated chord using any strumming rhythm that sounds good.)

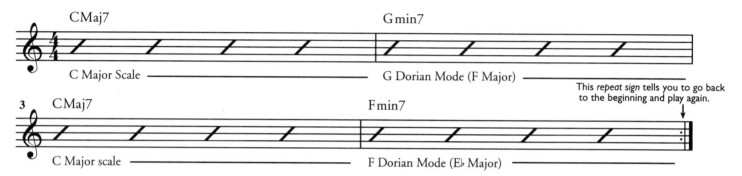

We can use a C Major scale over measure 1. In measure 2, however, there is a Gmin7 chord. This chord does not appear naturally in the key of C. If you've done your homework, you'll know that Gmin7 appears in the key of F as the ii chord. The Dorian mode corresponds to the ii chord in any key, so you can improvise using a G Dorian mode over measure 2. Gmin7 also appears as the iii chord in E♭ Major and the vi chord in B♭ Major. You can, and should, experiment with these sounds as well, but most jazz players would probably opt for the Dorian sounds. In measure 3, we go back to the C Major scale. Over the Fmin7 chord in measure 4, we can play F Dorian. Fmin7 appears as the ii chord in E♭ Major. As you can see, studying modes gives us many more scales to use when improvising.

The following example shows a simple *blues progression* (see page 124) in B♭. It is common to use all dominant 7th chords in a blues progression like this.

Every major key contains one dominant seventh chord—the V7 chord. All V7 chords correspond to the Mixolydian mode. So, over the B♭7 chord we can improvise using the B♭ Mixolydian mode—the fifth mode of the E♭ scale. Over the E♭7, we could use the E♭ Mixolydian mode—the fifth mode of the A♭ scale and over the F7, F Mixolydian would work, being the fifth mode of the B♭ scale.

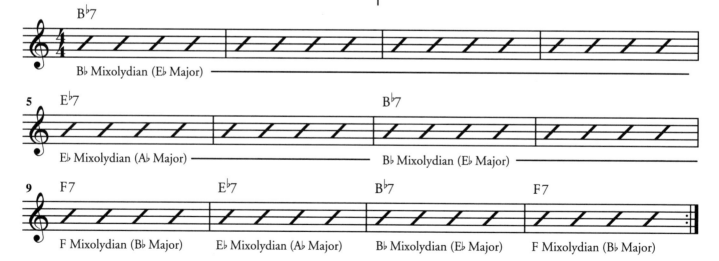

Sometimes this concept takes a little time to sink in. If working with modes is new for you, mull these concepts over a while before moving on.

Chapter 11: Altered Chords

There are many components used to make jazz sound like jazz, but one of the most important is the use of *altered chords*. Previously, we talked about building triads and 7th chords. These chords are the foundation of all music. Jazz music is often associated with "spicier" sounds. This spice comes from altering certain tones in certain chords.

Altered Dominant Chords

The chords that jazz players alter most often are dominant 7th chords.

Luckily, the formulas for the altered chords are inherent in the chord symbol itself, as you will see.

It is important to note that the most common notes to alter in any dominant chord are the 5th and the 9th. We can *lower* (or flat) a 5th or a 9th, or we can *raise* (sharp) a 5th or a 9th—and we can then combine these altered notes if we wish. This means that the following types of altered 7th chords are possible.

From a C root: C7♭5, C7♯5, C7♭9, C7♯9, C7♭9♭5, C7♯9♯5, C7♯9♭5 and C7♭9♯5. To construct any of these chords, simply start with the basic 7th chord and make the alterations described in the name.

You will also find dominant 9th and 13th chords with altered 5ths and 9ths, such as C9♯5 or C13♭9. Dominant chords with raised 11ths are also common. Just remember that a ♯11 is the same as a ♭5 one octave higher.

The following examples show common fingerings for many of these altered dominant chords.

31   **C7♭5 = R–3–♭5–♭7**

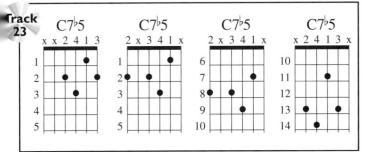

32   **C7♯5 = R–3–♯5–♭7**

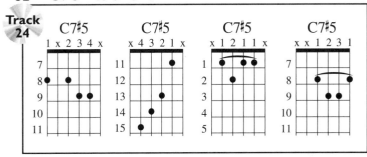

33   **C7♭9 = R–3–5–♭7–♭9**

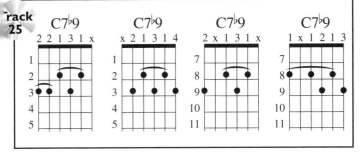

34   **C7♯9 = R–3–5–♭7–♯9**

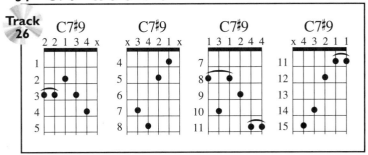

35   **C13♭9 = R–3–5–♭7–♭9–13**

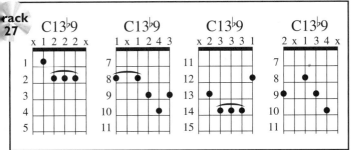

C7♭9♭5 = R–3–♭5–♭7–♭9

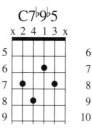
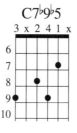

C7♯9♭5 = R–3–♭5–♭7–♯9

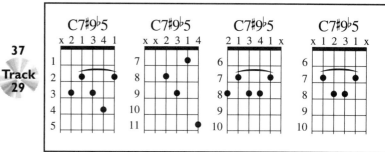

C7♯9♯5 = R–3–♯5–♭7–♯9

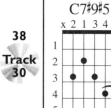
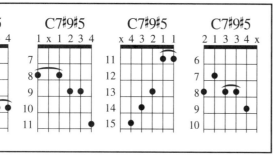

C7♭9♯5 = R–3–♯5–♭7–♭9

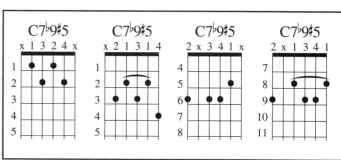

Altered Major Chords

Altered major chords are not used nearly as extensively as altered dominant chords. Maj7♯5 and Maj7♯11 are two that will pop up sometimes.

CMaj7♯5 = R–3–♯5–7

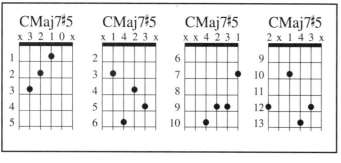

CMaj7♯11 = R–3–5–7–♯11 (or ♭5)

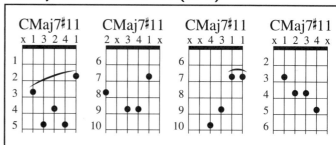

Altered Minor Chords

Minor 7th flat 5th chords are common. After all, they appear as the vii chord in all major keys. Minor 7th sharp 5th chords are less common, but you will see them from time to time.

Cmin7♭5 = R–♭3–♭5–♭7

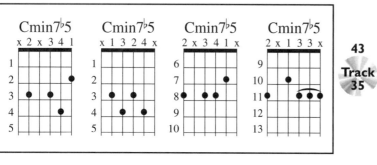

Cmin7♯5 = R–3–♯5–♭7

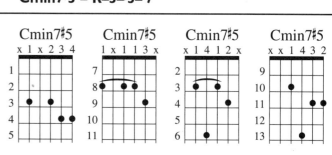

Chapter 12: The Minor Scales

The most important minor scales in Western harmony are the *natural*, *harmonic* and *melodic minor* scales. Let's analyze them in relation to each other.

The Natural Minor Scale

The *natural minor scale* is the same as the Aeolian mode of the major scale. By starting on the 6th degree of any major scale and moving one octave up the scale, we create a natural minor scale. The 6th degree of the major scale becomes the 1st degree of the natural minor scale. This results in a different formula of whole steps and half steps: Whole Step–Half Step–Whole Step–Whole Step–Half Step–Whole Step–Whole Step. Consequently, scale degrees 3, 6 and 7 are one half step lower than they would be in a major scale, making them ♭3, ♭6 and ♭7.

C Major Scale — 6th degree

A Natural Minor Scale — 1 2 ♭3 4 5 ♭6 ♭7 8

Here are six fingerings for the A Natural Minor scale. The tonics are highlighted. These are movable fingerings that you should learn in all 12 keys.

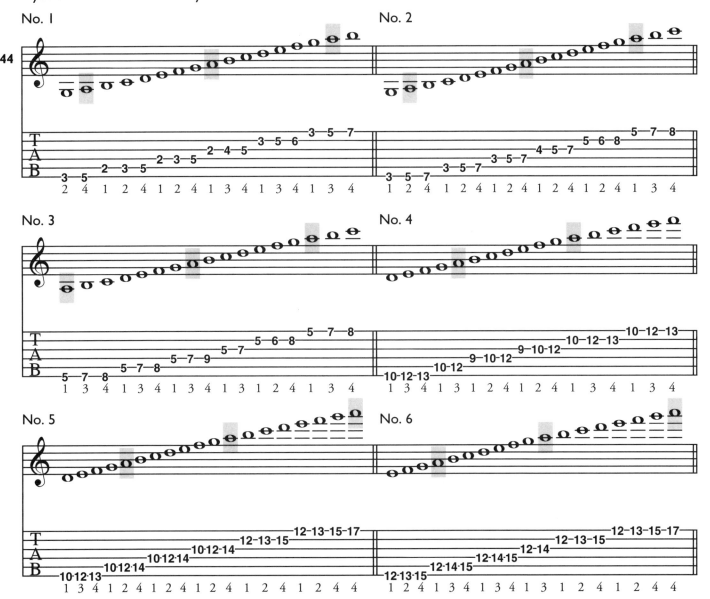

The Harmonic Minor Scale

When we want to create a *harmonic minor scale*, we simply start with a natural minor scale and then raise the 7th degree (which gives us a ♮7). Altering this one note produces a much more "exotic" sounding minor scale.

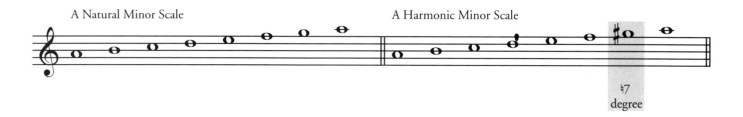

Below are six fingerings for an A Harmonic Minor scale.

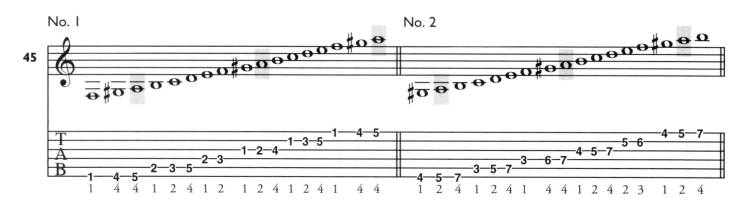

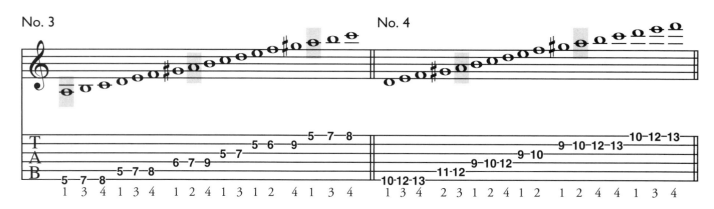

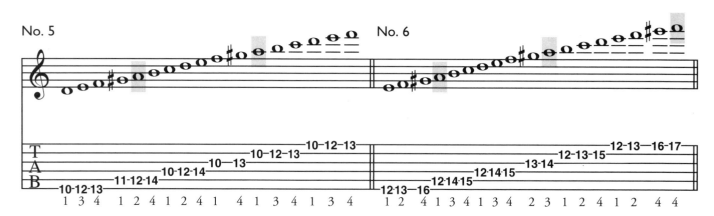

The Melodic Minor Scale

Once again, starting with a natural minor scale, we'll raise both the 6th and 7th degrees of the scale (giving us a ♮6 and ♮7) to produce a *melodic minor scale*.

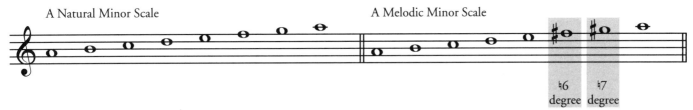

We can also create melodic minor scales by lowering the 3rd of any major scale:

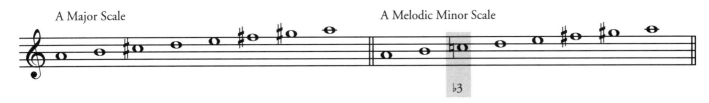

Below are six fingerings for melodic minor scales rooted on A.

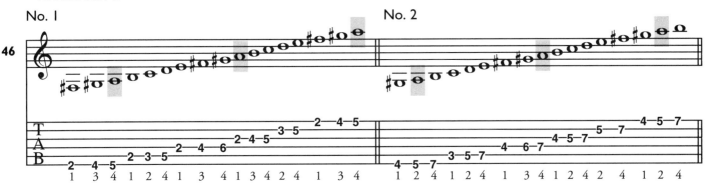

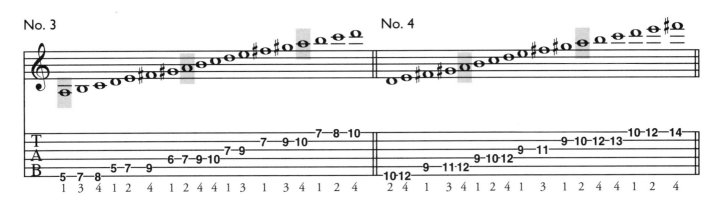

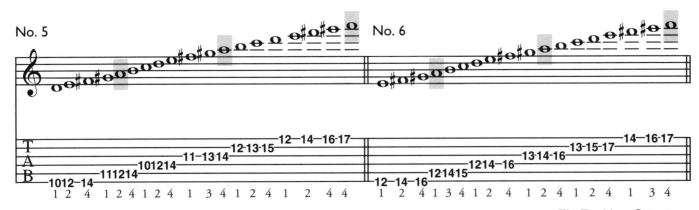

The Harmonized Minor Scales

Like the major scale, each minor scale produces a series of diatonic chords. Since there are three different minor scales, there are three different sets of diatonic minor chords. Music written in minor keys often combines the chords from all three minor scales, so it's a good idea to be familiar with each set.

The Harmonized Natural Minor Scale

Obviously, the chords produced by the natural minor scale are identical to those of the relative major scale because both scales contain the same notes. However, their Roman numerals change. The vi min7 of the major scale becomes i min7 of the minor scale, vii min7♭5 becomes ii min7♭5, and so on.

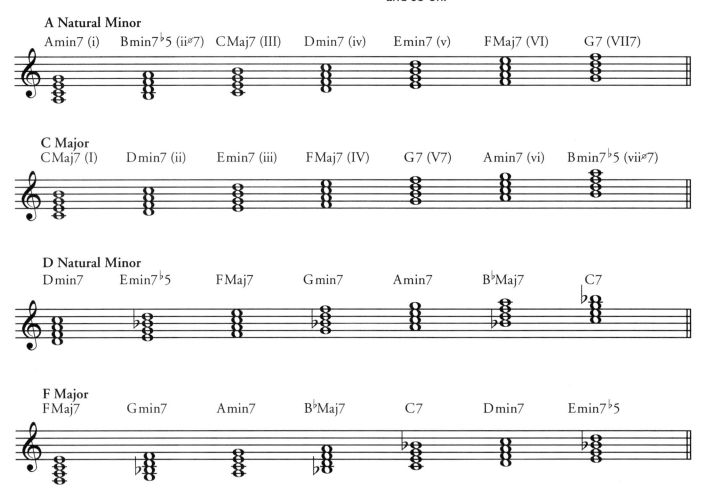

Following are two harmonized natural minor scales to play. Be sure to practice them from every root.

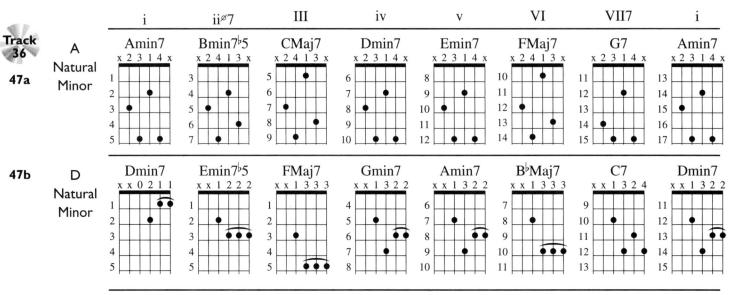

The Harmonized Harmonic Minor Scale

The raised 7th degree in this scale definitely changes the overall harmony from that of the natural minor scale.

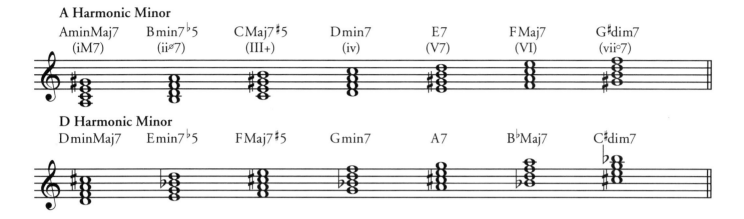

Here are two fingerings harmonizing the harmonic minor scale. Memorize and transpose to all keys.

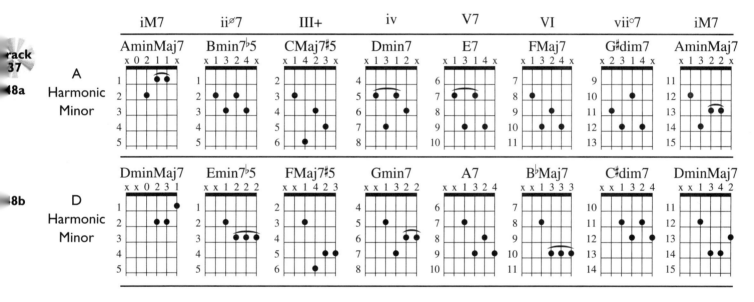

The Harmonized Melodic Minor Scale

Below are the chords produced by harmonizing the melodic minor scale. Once again, check out the unique harmonies and differences between the three minor scales.

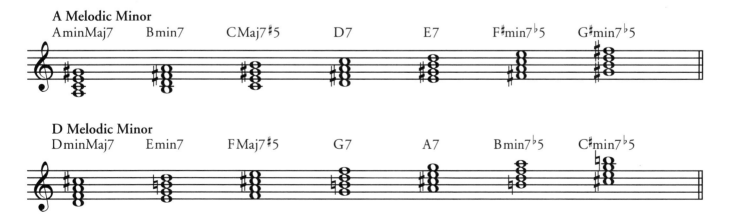

Here are some fingerings for the chords of the melodic minor scale:

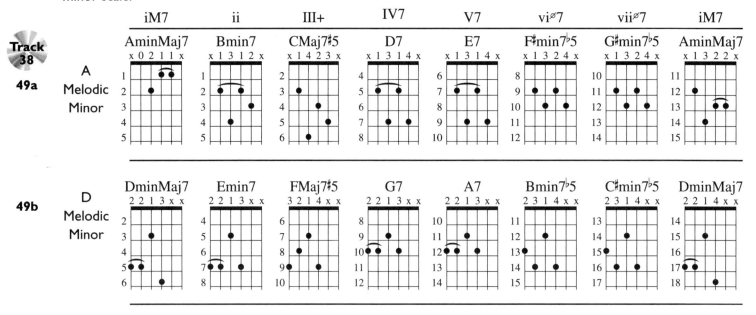

The Modes of the Minor Scales

Natural Minor Modes

You already know the modes of the natural minor scale, because they are based on the modes of the major scale. If you think of the natural minor scale as the Aeolian mode of the relative major scale, you will see that the 2nd mode is Locrian, the 3rd mode is Ionian, the 4th mode is Dorian, the 5th mode is Phrygian, the 6th mode is Lydian and the 7th mode is Mixolydian. (See page 48 to review the modes of the major scale.)

Harmonic Minor Modes

Once again, by creating modes from the harmonic minor scale, we generate new scales to use for improvising or composing. Like the modes of the major scale, each minor scale mode corresponds to the appropriate diatonic chord.

Following are the modes generated by the harmonic minor scale.

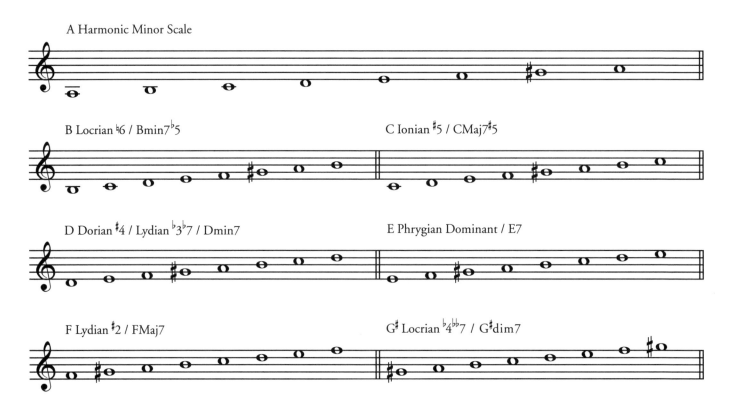

Melodic Minor Modes

Below are the modes of the melodic minor scale. Some modes are used more than others. Many will be discussed later in this book when we begin improvising over actual chord progressions.

A Melodic Minor Scale

B Dorian ♭2 / Bmin7

C Lydian Augmented / CMaj7#5

D Lydian ♭7 / D7

E Mixolydian ♭6 / E7

F# Locrian #2 / F#min7♭5

G# Super Locrian* / G#min7♭5

* See page 67 for an explanation of the Super Locrian mode.

Chapter 13: The ii–V7–I Progression

In jazz, the ii–V7–I progression (pronounced "two five one") is the most common and important chord progression because its sound establishes the key of the I chord. In order to understand this more clearly, it might be helpful to think of the I chord in any key as sort of a magnet. All of the diatonic chords in a key have varying levels of attraction back to the I chord.

In the key of B♭, if you play an F7 chord by itself, your ear feels unsatisfied. If you follow that F7 with a B♭ Major chord, there is a feeling of *resolution*. The ii–V7–I progression implies the key center in a powerful way because of the harmonic momentum set up by the ii and V7 chords along with the "pull" of the I chord on them. The diatonic chords in a key want to return to I, but they also have an attraction to other chords in the key (and sometimes outside the key) as well. The example below shows some of the most common chord movements.

Chord	Attraction
I	Establishes the key center
ii	Moves to V7 or ♭ii
iii	Moves to vi or ♭iii
IV	Moves to V7 or I
V7	Moves to I
vi	Moves to ii or ♭vi
vii	Moves to I, iii or ♭vii

Below is a list of all 12 diatonic ii–V7–I progressions. Be sure to memorize them.

Key	ii	V7	I
C	Dmin7	G7	CMaj7
F	Gmin7	C7	FMaj7
B♭	Cmin7	F7	B♭Maj7
E♭	Fmin7	B♭7	E♭Maj7
A♭	B♭min7	E♭7	A♭Maj7
D♭	E♭min7	A♭7	D♭Maj7
G♭	A♭min7	D♭7	G♭Maj7
B	C♯min7	F♯7	BMaj7
E	F♯min7	B7	EMaj7
A	Bmin7	E7	AMaj7
D	Emin7	A7	DMaj7
G	Amin7	D7	GMaj7

Extending or Altering Chords

In jazz harmony, it is usually considered "legal" to extend or alter any chord so long as the extension or alteration does not conflict with the melody in any way.

In other words:

- Dmin7 could be replaced with a Dmin9, Dmin11, Dmin6 or Dmin13.
- A CMaj7 could be changed to CMaj9 or C6.
- Dominant chords like G7 could not only be extended to include a 9th, 11th or 13th, but could also contain altered tones like the ♭5, ♯5, ♭9 or ♯9.

So, in actuality our ii–V7–I progression that started out as Dmin7–G7–CMaj7 could be transformed into:

- Dmin9–G13–CMaj13, or
- Dmin11–G13♭9–C6, or
- Dmin–G7♭5–CMaj9, or
- any other variation that sounds good to you.

There is a lot of freedom in jazz.

Importance of the ii and V7

Many songs in the standard jazz repertoire consist of various ii–V7–I progressions traveling through many keys. It is important to note that the ii and the V7 chord will still establish the key center regardless of whether the I chord is present or not.

As you will see, this situation is commonplace. The following example shows two typical chord progressions that illustrate this point.

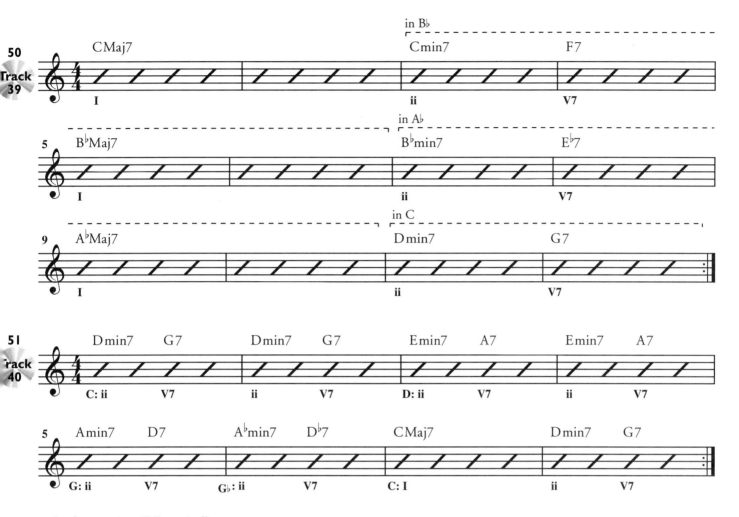

Minor ii–V7–i Progressions

In minor keys, the minor ii–V7–i progression is very common, and you will often find them sandwiched in songs that are in major keys as well.

The ii chord is generally a half-diminished chord. The V7 can be an unaltered dominant chord, but it commonly is played as a V7♭9 chord. The i chord is generally a minor 7th chord.

The following example shows a typical chord progression that contains both major ii–V7–I and minor ii–V7–i progressions. Play through this example and get to know the sound of each kind of progression.

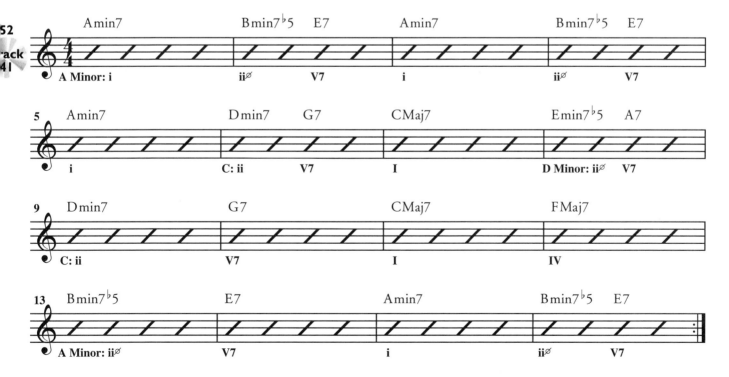

Chapter 14: Applying Neighbor Tones

If you have been improvising using the major scale only, you have no doubt noticed the "vanilla" quality of its sound. You may be wondering where all the "spicy" sounds lie. Actually, there are many places these sounds can be found.

One of the simplest ways to add *chromaticism* (notes outside the major scale, one source of spiciness) to your improvised lines is by using *neighbor tones*. Neighbor tones are the notes that surround chord tones. One of the reasons you learned your arpeggio fingerings was so that you could "spell out" the chord changes in your solos. This is all well and good, but now it's time to really highlight these chord tones. Using neighbor tones is an excellent way to accomplish this. By far, the most common neighbor tones are the notes one half step below and one half step above the chord tones. Neighbor tones a whole step above and below are also common.

The neighbor tone technique requires that you look ahead in your solo. The targeted chord tones are generally played on strong beats of the measure, so it is important to apply neighbor tones either one beat or one half beat before the chord tone. The examples below feature a neighbor tone one half beat before beat 1 of measure 1 (known as the *downbeat*). Using neighbor tones is a great way to emphasize chord changes and extend the length of your lines (the melodies that you spontaneously improvise).

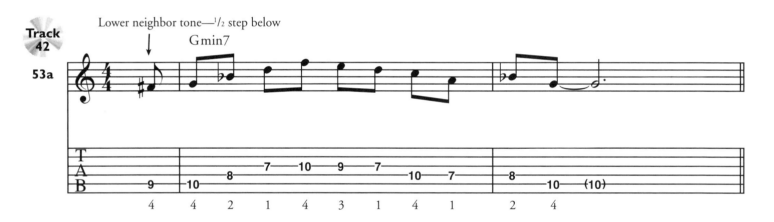

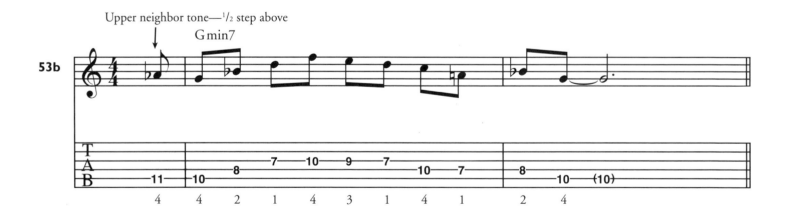

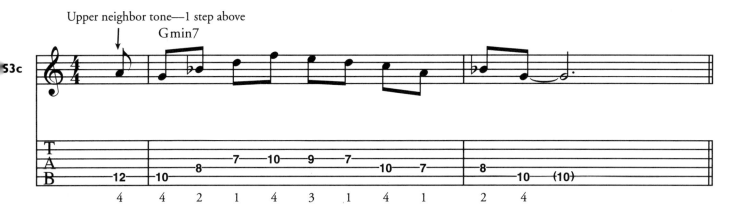

You can also use combinations of neighbor tones as in the examples below.

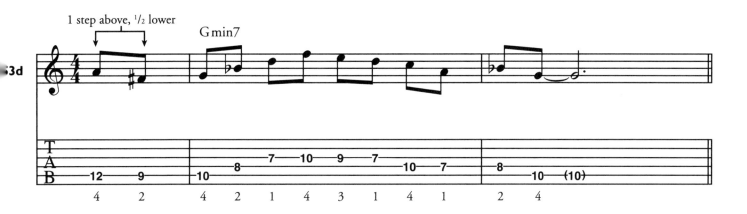

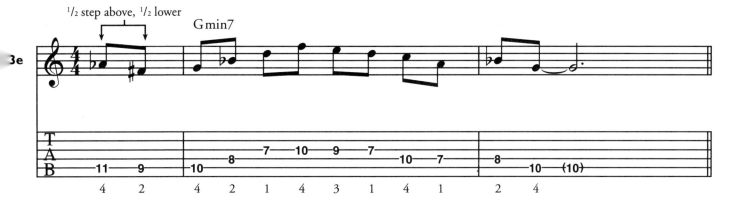

Chapter 15: Altered Scales

Another way to introduce chromaticism into your solos is by using various *altered scales*. There are quite a few to choose from, and one could easily spend a lifetime looking for and studying these kinds of scales. In the following sections, you'll be introduced to three altered scales that most players consider essential. In order to get you up and improvising as quickly as possible, only the most essential theory will be discussed. If you love theory and want to look at all these scales from various vantage points, you'll find this information readily available in my earlier books (see page 5 for a partial list).

Altered scales are primarily used to improvise over altered chords. Not all scales "fit" all altered chords, so you do need to discover which ones work in different situations.

The Diminished Scale

The diminished scale is a *symmetrical scale* (a scale whose notes divide the octave into equal parts) whose formula is: Whole Step–Half Step–Whole Step–Half Step–Whole Step–Half Step–Whole Step–Half Step.

C Diminished Scale

The diminished scale is useful in two different applications. As you would guess from the name, it can be used to improvise over diminished chords. In this case, you use the diminished scale that shares the root of the diminished chord you wish to improvise over.

The second application of the diminished scale is to improvise over altered chords. In the case of altered chords, we start this scale one-half step above the root of the altered chord in question. In other words, we would use an A♭ Diminished scale over an altered G7 chord, a D♭ Diminished scale over an altered (alt) C7 chord, and so on.

To find out exactly which altered chord the diminished scale works with, it is useful to write the scale out and analyze how each degree of the scale relates to the chord.

In the example below, we see an A♭ Diminished scale used over an altered G7 chord. We can see that in this case, the A♭ Diminished scale provides us with a ♭9, ♯9 and ♭5 of a G7 chord. This means that this scale can be used to improvise over the following altered G7 chords: G7♭9, G7♯9, G7♭5, G7♯11 (same as ♭5), G7♭5♭9 and G7♭5♯9.

A♭ Diminished scale over G7alt

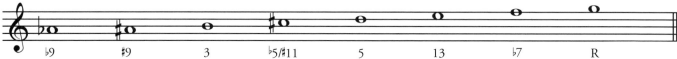

One of the cool things about diminished scale fingerings is that you can move them around the fretboard in minor 3rds and they will always contain the same notes, so you can use the diminished scale all over the fretboard quite easily.

Check out the fingerings that follow:

"A" Diminished Scale Fingerings

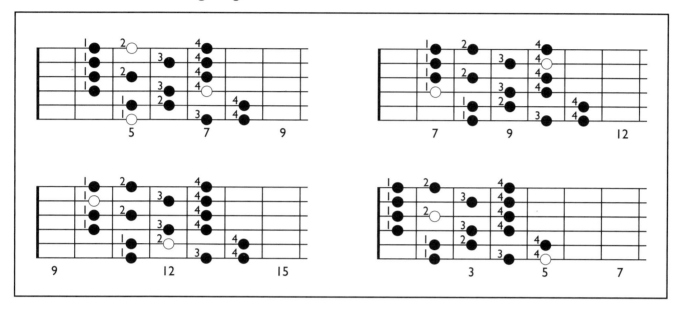

Altered dominant chords are commonly used as V7 chords in ii–V7–I progressions. This example shows how well a C♯ Diminished scale works over the C7♭5 chord in this ii–V7–I progression in F.

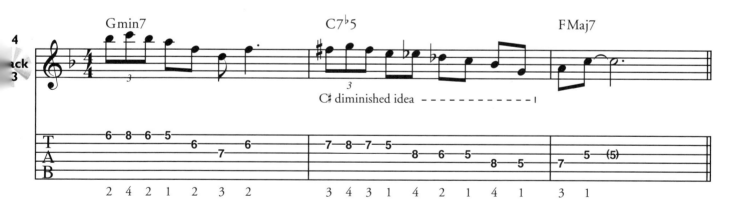

The Whole Tone Scale

The *whole tone scale* is another useful scale to use over altered dominant chords. Simply start it on the root of the chord.

Here is how the G whole tone scale stacks up over an altered G7 chord:

G Whole Tone scale over G7

We now see that the whole tone scale can be used over a G7♭5 (or ♯11), G7♯5, G9♭5 or G9♯5 chord.

Below are three fingerings for the whole tone scale to work with.

Whole Tone Scale Fingerings

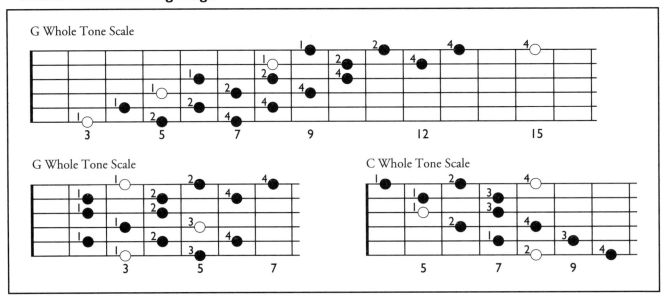

Here is an example of whole tone scale usage in a ii–V7–I progression in C.

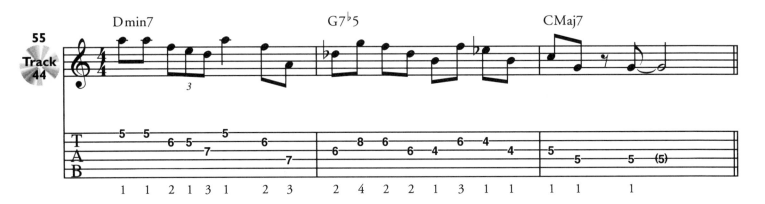

The Super Locrian Mode

The *super Locrian* mode is actually the seventh mode of the melodic minor scale and goes by a few different names. You'll hear players refer to it as the *diminished-whole tone scale*, the *altered scale* or as simply "playing the melodic minor scale one half-step above the root of the altered chord."

Below, we see that this scale contains every possible alteration of a dominant chord.

Super Locrian mode over G7

R   ♭9   ♯9   3   ♭5/♯11   ♯5   ♭7   R

So this scale will work over any dominant chord that contains a ♭5 (or ♯11), ♯5, ♭9, ♯9 or any combination of these. Pretty useful, but you'll find that you'll have to recognize the sound of all these alterations so that you can emphasize them within the scale. This takes time and practice, so have patience.

Below are a couple of good fingerings.

"G" Super Locrian Mode Fingerings

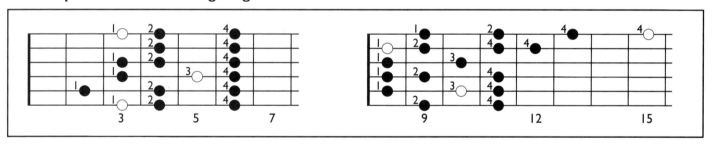

Following is an example of what this scale can sound like over a ii–V7–I in C.

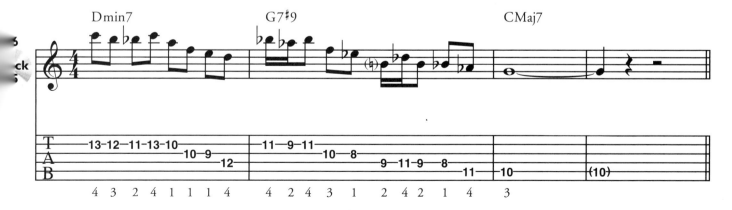

Chapter 16: Turnarounds

A *turnaround* is a two or four-measure section at a first ending or at the end of a tune. Turnarounds create a smooth harmonic transition back to the first measure. Most songs utilize turnarounds, so you'll eventually need quite a collection of them. They tend to make a chord progression much more interesting and generally help the tune to flow in a more attractive way. The turnarounds that follow are quite useable in most situations but should be thought of as only the start of your "collection." They are in the key of C, but be sure to transpose them to all keys so you can use them any time, in any context.

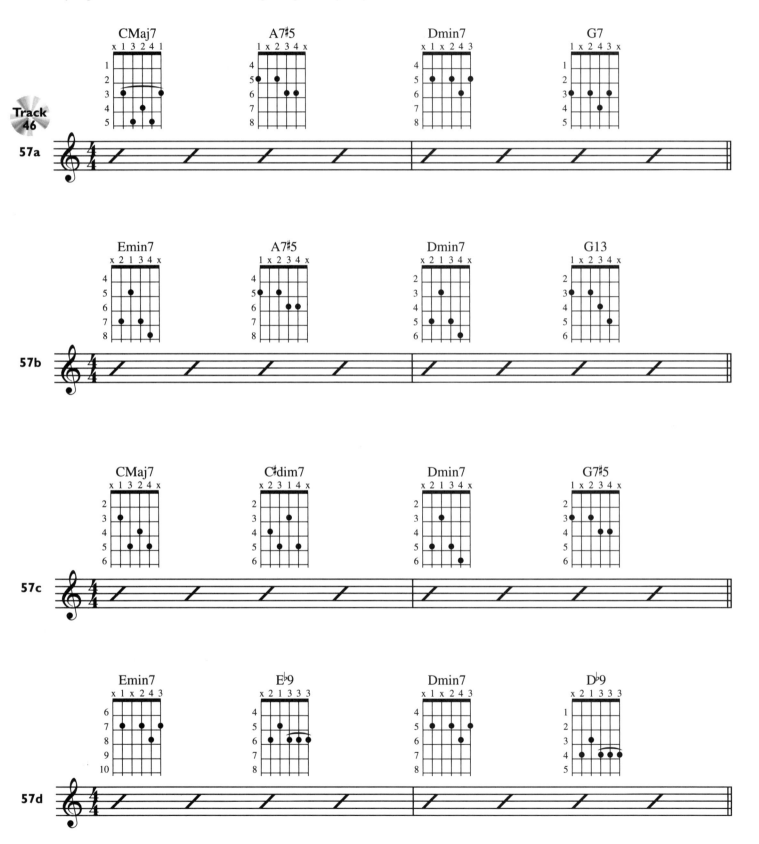

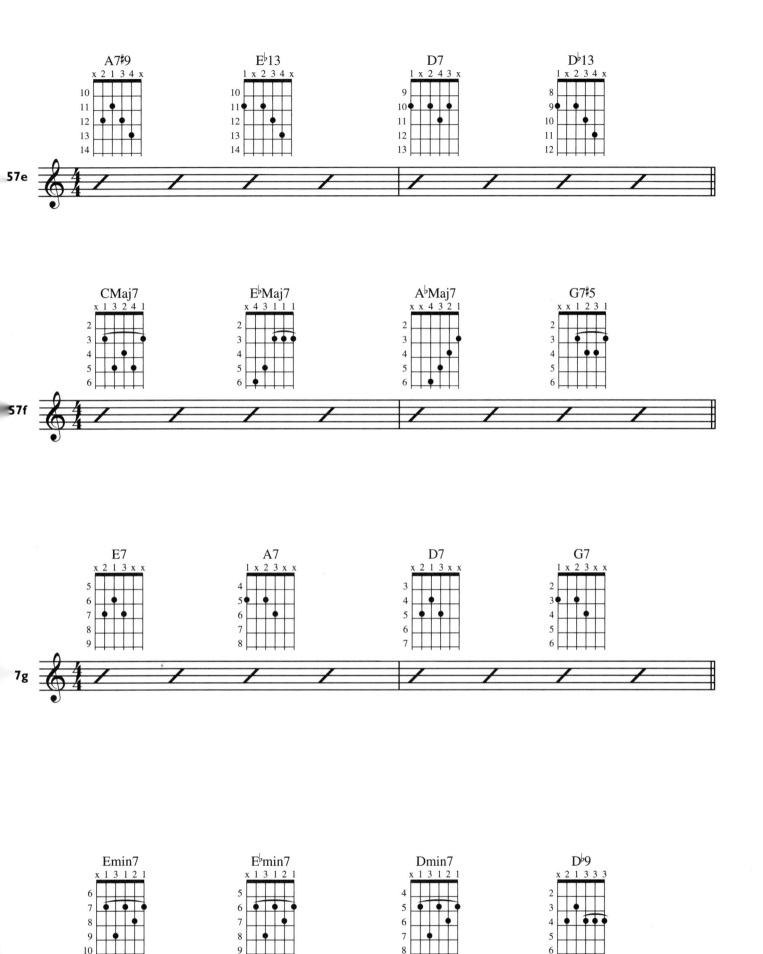

PART 2: Learning Tunes

Jazz musicians learn songs in a very different manner than most other kinds of players. Because jazz musicians improvise so much of the time, they must know many different ways to play the same song. For instance, you must be comfortable playing the melody of a song in different registers and possibly different keys as well. You must also know the harmonic progression of the song backward, forward and inside out and be able to comp the chord changes in any register. All this and many other concepts like chord substitution and reharmonization, as well as a variety of arranging techniques all go into the successful execution of a jazz performance.

Since space is limited in any book, this section will focus on how to really *know* a tune. We will concentrate on the following areas:

1. **Jazz performance in a group where there is another harmonic instrument such as a keyboard or another guitar.** When playing with a keyboardist or guitarist, it is common to play melodies in single notes and let the other player take care of the harmonic choices. Although there are many examples of guitars and keyboards co-existing in harmonic bliss, it is usually best to divide the melodic and harmonic duties.

2. **Jazz performance in which the guitar is the primary harmonic and lead instrument.** In this situation, the guitarist generally plays in a chord melody style while playing the *head* (another name for the song's melody, typically played at the beginning and end of the performance) of the song. There will be a sample chord melody arrangement for each of the songs that follow.

3. **Improvisational ideas.** Each song will show an example of an improvised *chorus* (one time through the song's form) with some analysis.

In all three areas, a firm understanding of the melody and chords is absolutely essential, so in every song that follows we will discuss and show:

1. Ways to play the melody in single notes using various areas of the fretboard.

2. Chordal ideas in six different regions of the fretboard.

Please keep in mind that the material ahead is only a beginning. In truth, you could spend many years working in only one of these areas for any given song. This "endless" task is actually part of the fun and challenge that keeps jazz players so interested in this music. In other words, you never really finish. You will always find new ways to play any song, and each new song you learn will provide new challenges for you.

What is intended in this part of the book is to show an approach to learning tunes that you'll be able to use for many years.

There is good news, and there is bad news. The bad news is that the first few tunes to which you apply these methods will take quite a while to master. The good news is that after you've finished a few songs in this way, newer tunes will not take nearly as long to master because most songs have many components in common. Hang in there and know that things will get easier. This methodology has worked with literally thousands of students over many years.

Let's dig in.

Chapter 17: "I'm in the Mood for Love"

The first song we're going to look at is "I'm in the Mood for Love," which is an older standard by Jimmy McHugh and Dorothy Fields. It has been recorded many times by artists in jazz as well as other genres.

There are certain things you should know before putting together a new song.

1. **How many measures is the tune?**
   In this song there are 32 measures, which is incredibly common in songs of this type.

2. **What is the song's form?**
   In other words, how are those 32 measures arranged? In most 32 measure songs the form is A–A–B–A. This means that the song is divided up into four eight-bar sections. The first section (A) is eight measures long. Often, those same eight measures are repeated (hence, the second A section). At the end of the first A section, there is usually a turnaround that brings you back to the beginning of the second A section. The second A section will generally have a different ending, providing a feeling of finality before moving on to the B section. The B section is usually quite different both melodically and harmonically from the A sections, which gives a feeling of movement. The final A section is usually a repeat of the second A section with possibly a different final ending. Keep in mind that there are exceptions to this description, but you'll find that most songs of this type will follow this pattern.

   Below are some terms and symbols you will see in written music to help you follow the form of a tune.

   - **Coda**—This is an ending to a piece of music. The **Coda** symbol is ⊕.

   - **D.C. al Coda** (Da Capo al Coda) tells you to repeat from the beginning of the piece and play to the **Coda** symbol ⊕, at which point you jump to the **Coda.**

   - **D.S. al Coda** (Dal Segno al Coda) tells you to repeat from the **D.S.** symbol 𝄋 and play on until you come to the **Coda** symbol ⊕, at which point you jump to the **Coda.**

   - **D.C. al Fine** tells you to repeat from the beginning and play to the word **Fine** (pronounced fee-nay), where you end the piece.

   - **D.S. al Fine** tells you to repeat from the **D.S.** symbol 𝄋 and play on until you come to the word **Fine,** where you end.

3. **In what key is the song?**
   In this song, the key is C Major. Most jazz tunes *modulate* through several keys (leaving the tune's original diatonic harmony behind to temporarily explore new tonalities), but the key signature will still designate the song's key. You need to know this so you can tell your bandmates what key you'll be playing in.

4. **What is the feel of the song?**
   In mainstream jazz, the four most common feels would be swing, Latin, ballad or straight-eighth note feels. You certainly don't have to play with the same feel every time you play the song, but for the purpose of putting a song together for the first time, it might be a good idea to establish a general feel. For this song, we'll be using a medium tempo *swing feel.*

In *swing* music, eighth notes are played with a triplet feel. The best way to learn how to swing is to listen to the jazz masters.

Learning the Melody

It is important to be able to play the melody of the song in at least two different octaves. Of course, on the guitar it is often possible to play melodies in more than one location encompassing identical octaves. All possibilities should be explored until you settle on the most comfortable locations, or the ones that produce the best sound. Since this song is in the key of C, you might want to try playing the melody within a few of the C Major scale fingerings you know. You should be aware that oftentimes the best and most uniform sound is accomplished by playing up and down a single string.

This example shows a fingering for the melody in the octave in which it was originally written. It should be memorized.

Note that there is a *1st ending* and a *2nd ending* in the music. This means that you play all the way through the 1st ending, then repeat from the beginning. On the second pass through the music, jump over the 1st ending to the 2nd ending and play to the end.

Track 47

I'M IN THE MOOD FOR LOVE
(Melody in Single Notes)

McHugh/Fields

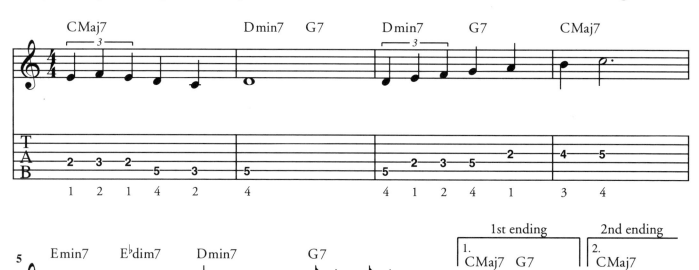

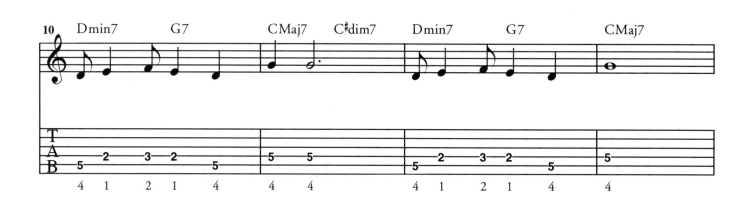

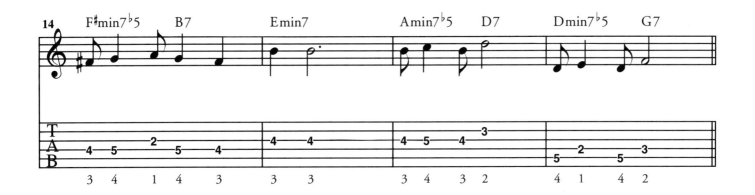

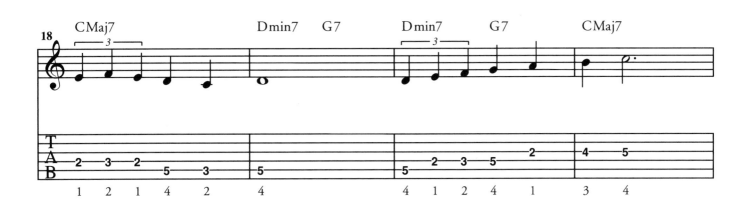

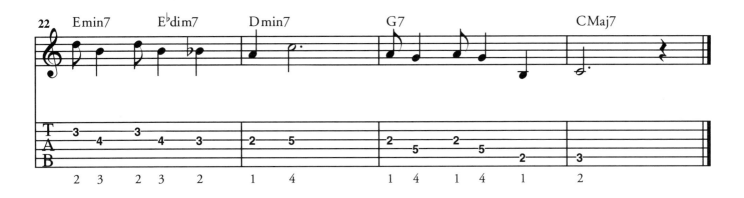

Here is a fingering for the melody one octave higher than written. Memorize it.

I'M IN THE MOOD FOR LOVE
(Melody One Octave Higher)

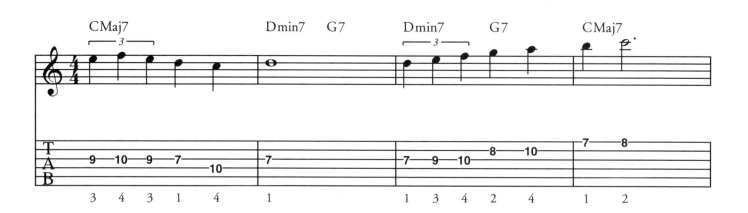

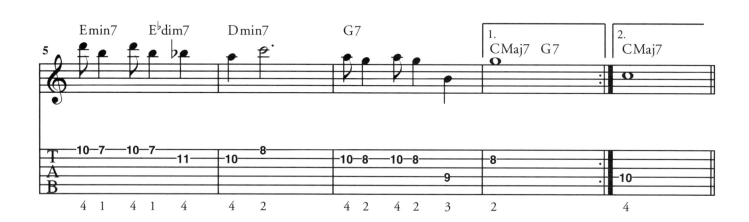

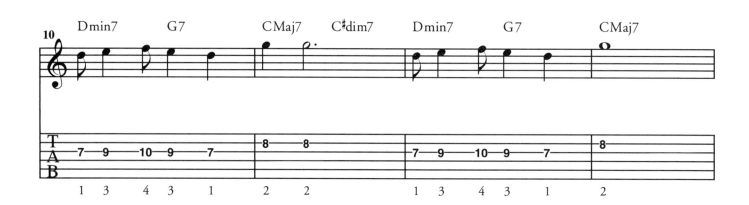

Working on the Changes

Now that you have learned the melody using a couple of different fingerings and octaves, it's time to learn the chord changes. In Chapter 13 (page 60), we discussed how chord progressions in jazz often follow various patterns of ii–V7–I progressions. Be sure you analyze this song in this way. Just get familiar with where the ii–V7–I progressions lie. Also, become aware of the chord changes that seem to lie outside of any ii–V7–I situation. You will need to do this before we talk about improvising over this tune.

Remember that to most jazz musicians there are three main families of chords (major, minor and dominant), and that any chord can be replaced with another chord from its own family. In other words, a CMaj7 chord can be replaced with a C6, CMaj9, CMaj13 or any other major type chord with a C root. The same is true for minor and dominant chords as well. The only time you cannot do this is when a particular chord interferes or "clashes" with the melody or soloist.

We now have a big job ahead of us. The idea is to discover all the useable chords for this progression over the entire fretboard, and then practice using these chords in our song.

To make our approach more organized, we will divide the fretboard into six regions. These regions will use various frets and string sets and are described as follows:

Region 1—All six strings from open strings through the 5th fret.

Region 1

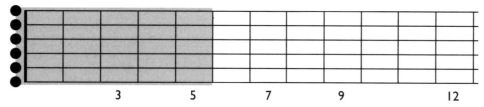

Region 2—All six strings from the 5th fret through the 9th fret.

Region 2

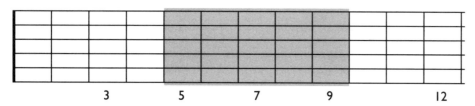

Region 3—All six strings from the 8th fret through the 12th fret.

Region 3

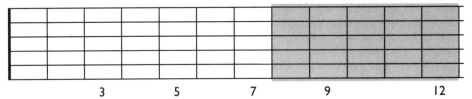

Region 4—The top four strings spanning the entire fretboard.

Region 4

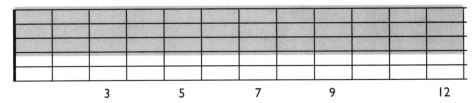

Region 5—The middle four strings spanning the entire fretboard.

Region 5

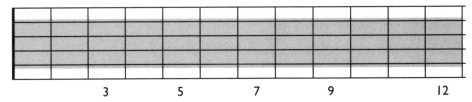

Region 6—The bottom four strings spanning the entire fretboard.

Region 6

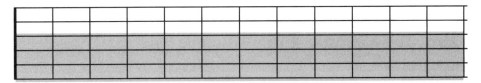

It should be noted that in Regions 4, 5 and 6, fewer than four strings can be used if desired. Also, songs in certain keys may necessitate modifying these regions slightly. If you need to extend a region by a fret now and then, go for it. Remember, there is a lot of freedom in jazz.

Region 1

Now, since the first chord in our song is a C Major type chord, we need to find all the C Major type fingerings in Region 1. Keep in mind that there are more possibilities here than could ever be listed in any book—we'll just look at a sample of chords—don't worry, though, you'll find plenty to work with.

C Major Type

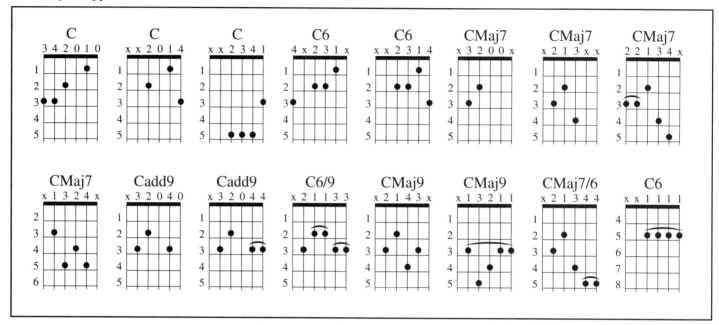

The next two chords we'll need are D Minor and G dominant type chords. Take a look at these:

D Minor Type

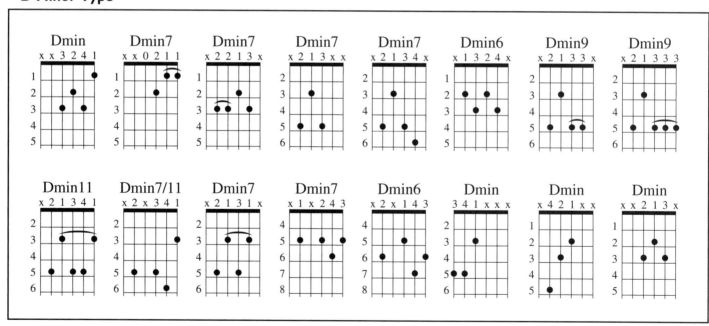

G Dominant Type

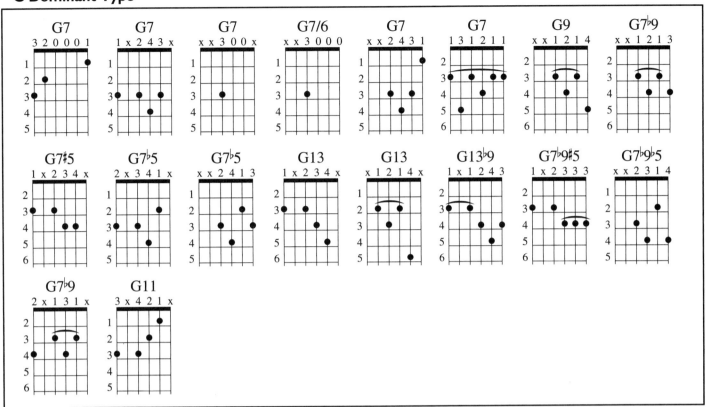

Below are some E Minor type chords and a few
E♭dim7 chords.

E Minor Type

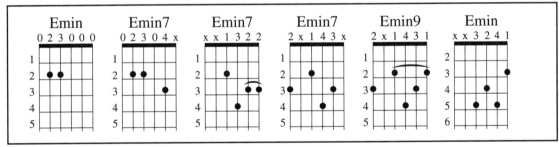

E♭dim7

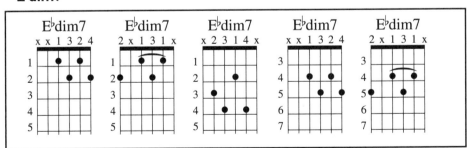

Alright, that takes care of all three A sections of the song's form. Now let's explore the changes of the B section, or *bridge* (the middle section of the tune that provides contrast to the A section). We see that there are six more new chords to look for. The remaining chords in the bridge are repeats of chords we already found in the A sections.

C#dim7

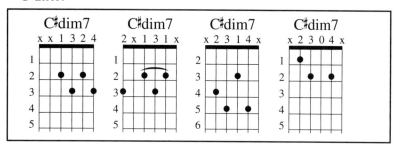

F#min7♭5

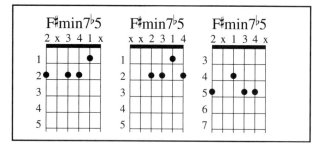

B Dominant Type

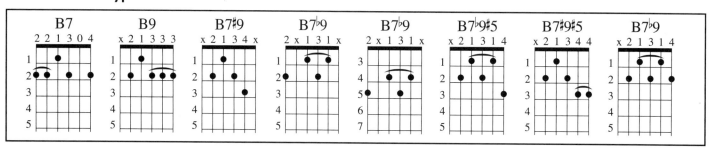

Amin7♭5

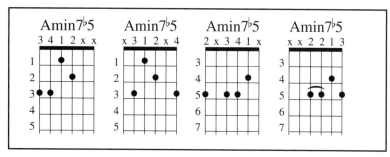

D Dominant Type

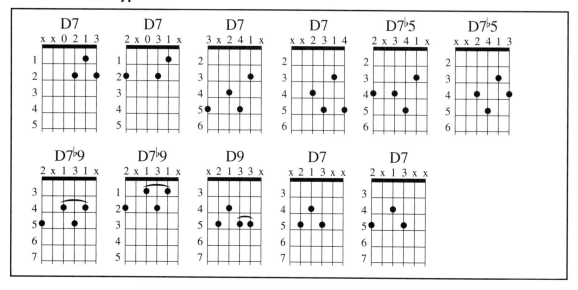

Dmin7♭5

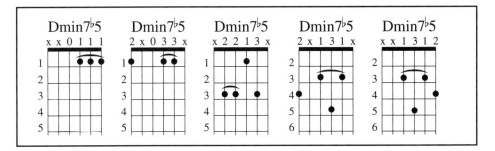

Alright, let's move on to Region 2.

Region 2
C Major Type

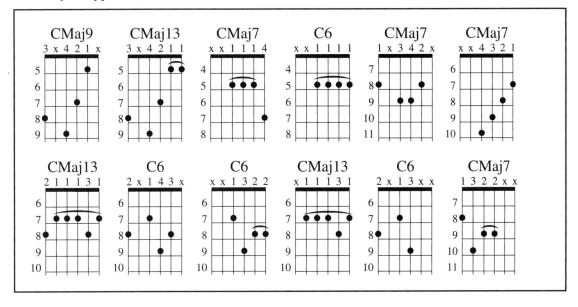

D Minor Type

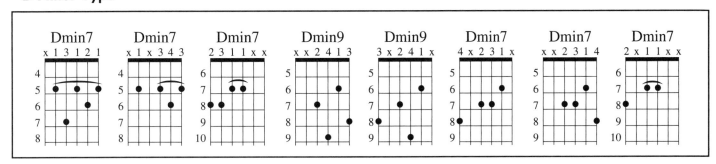

G Dominant Type

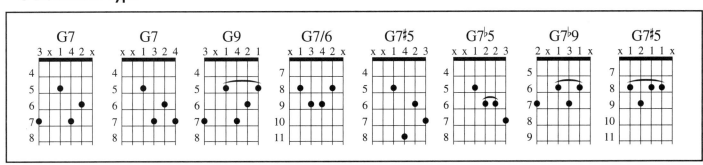

E Minor Type

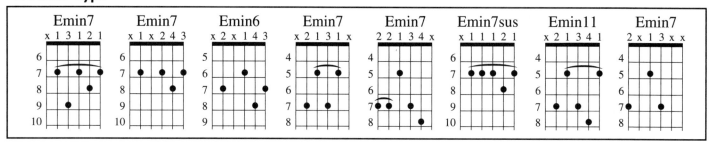

E♭dim7

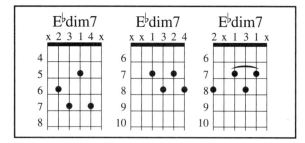

C#dim7

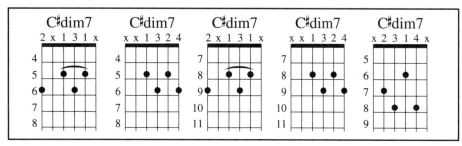

F#min7♭5

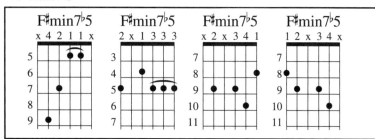

B Dominant Type

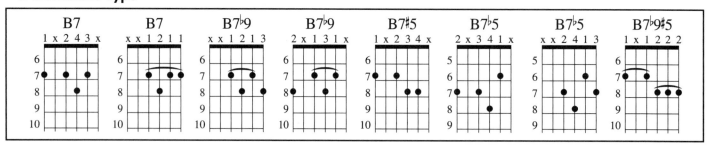

Amin7♭5

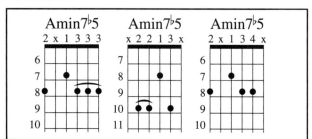

D Dominant Type

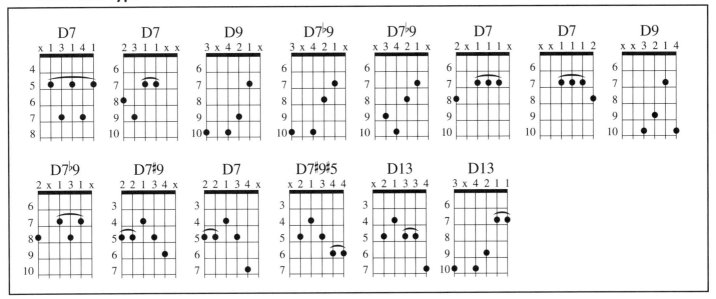

Dmin7♭5

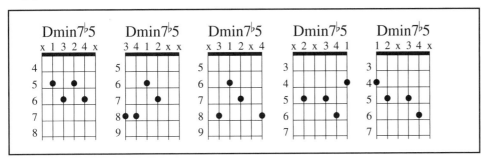

Region 3
C Major Type

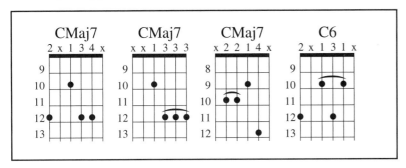

D Minor Type

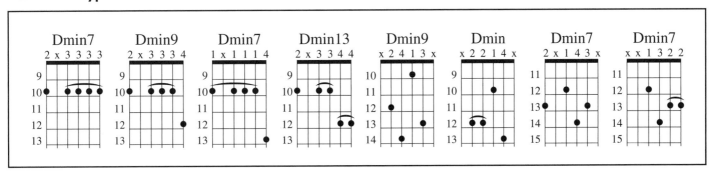

G Dominant Type

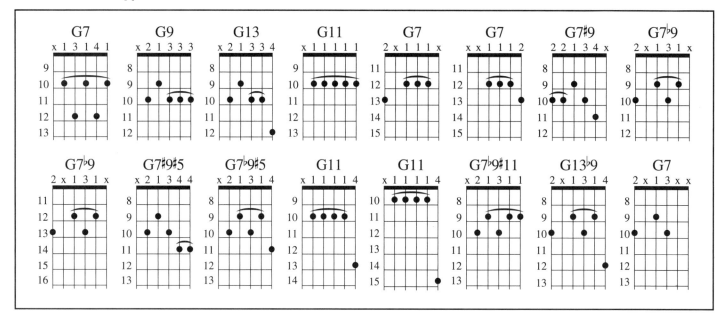

E Minor Type

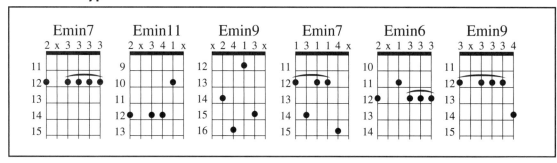

E♭dim7

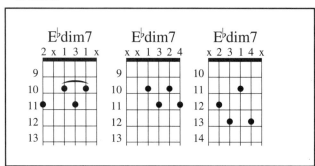

C♯dim7

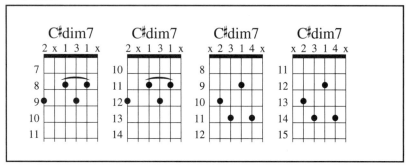

F#min7♭5

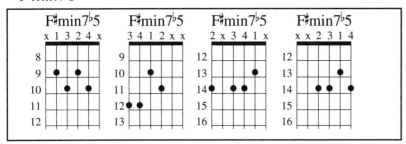

B Dominant Type

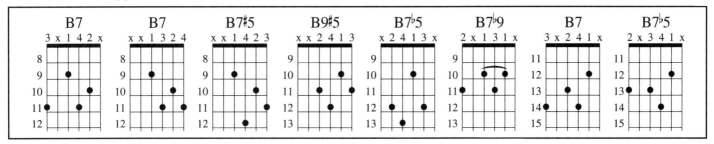

Amin7♭5

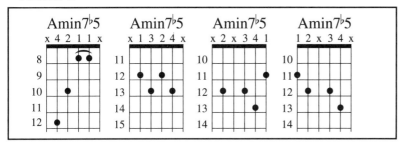

D Dominant Type

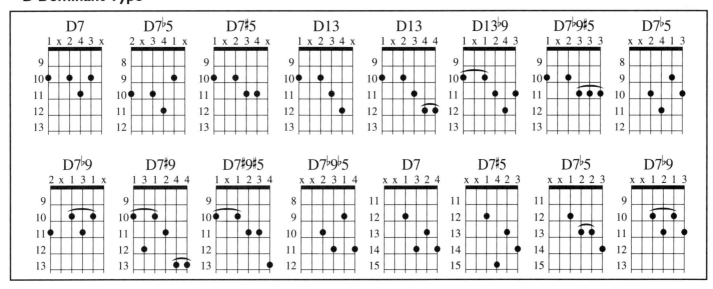

Dmin7♭5

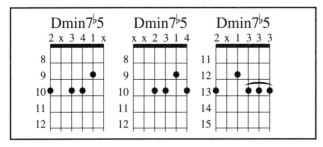

Region 4

C Major Type

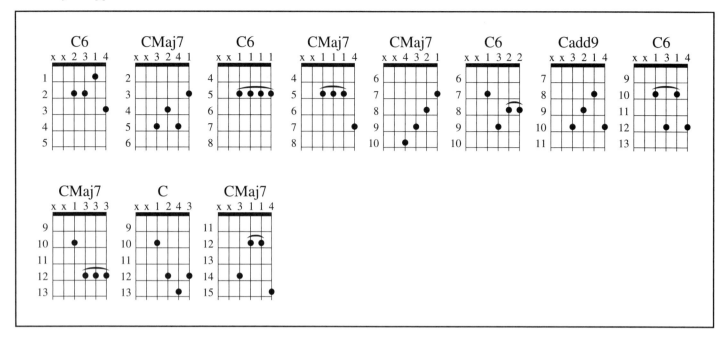

D Minor Type

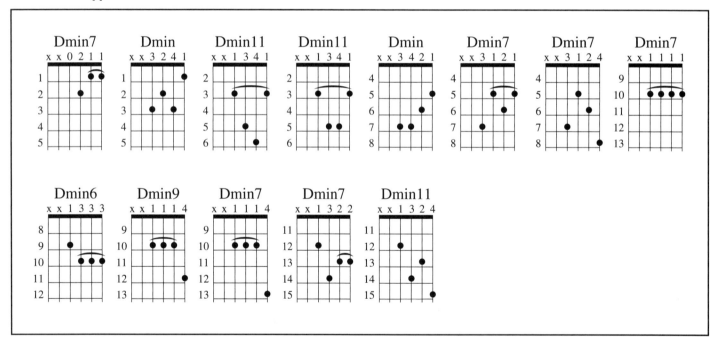

G Dominant Type

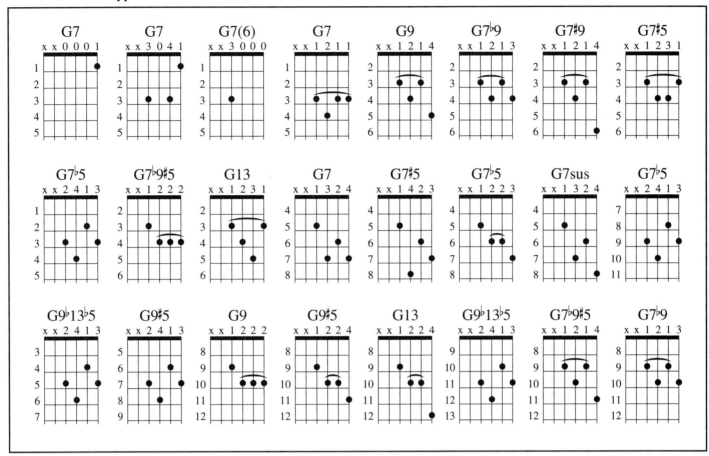

E Minor Type

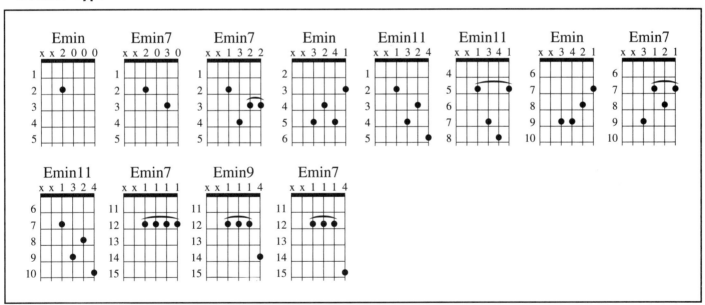

E♭dim7

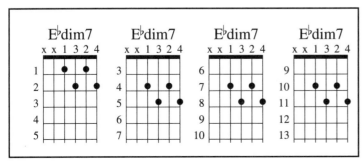

C#dim7

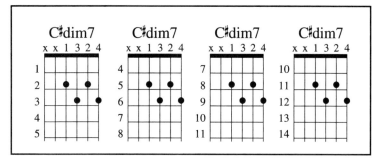

F#min7♭5

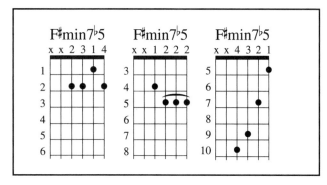

B Dominant Type

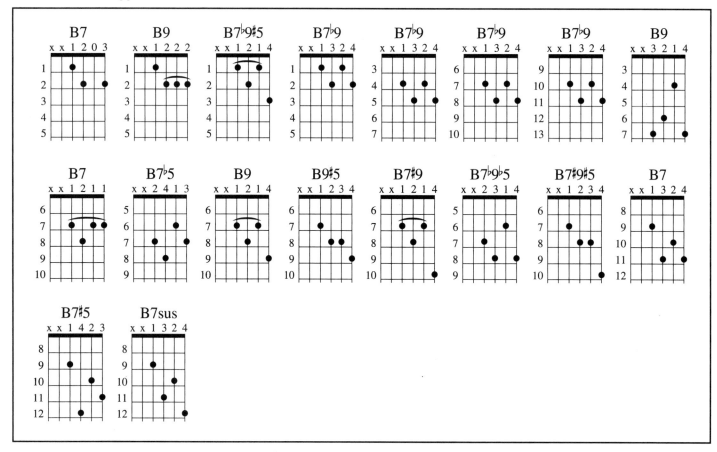

Amin7♭5

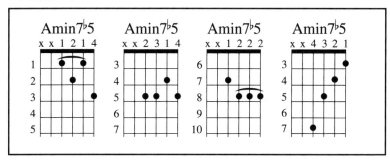

D Dominant Type

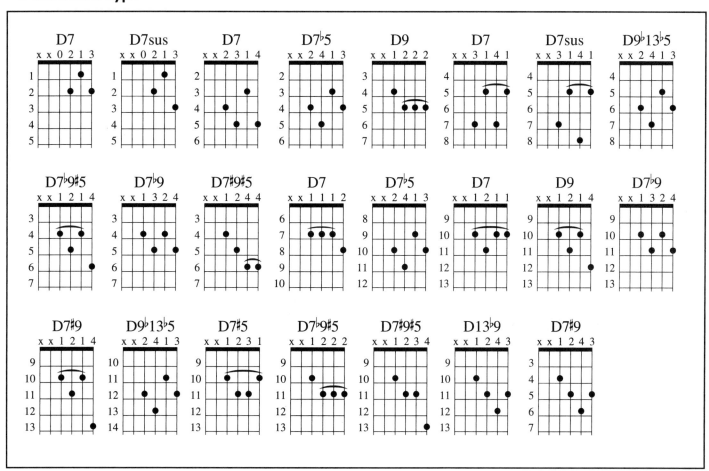

Dmin7♭5

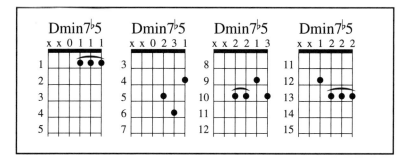

Region 5

C Major Type

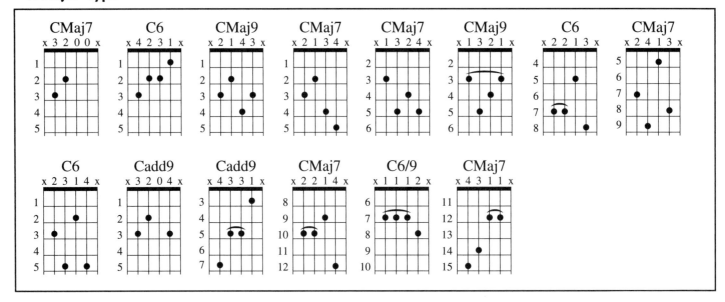

D Minor Type

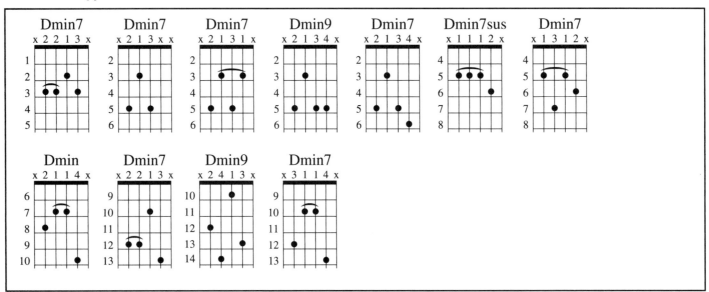

G Dominant Type

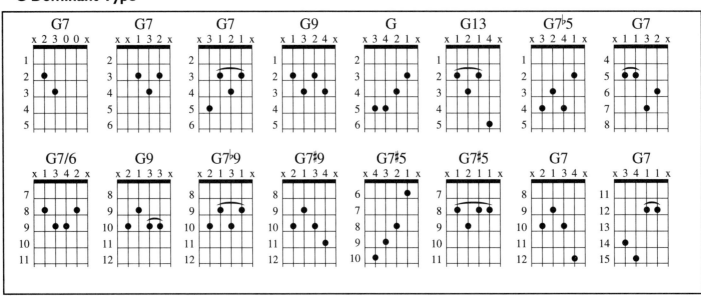

E Minor Type

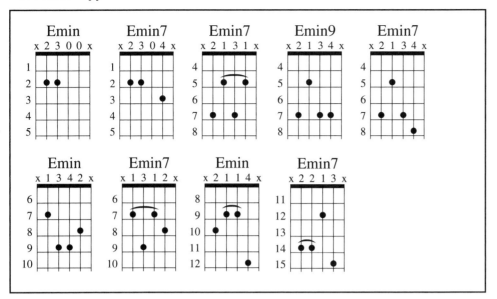

E♭dim7

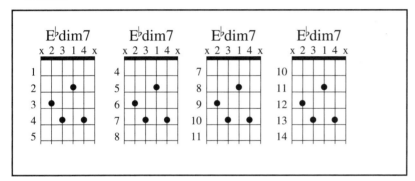

C♯dim7

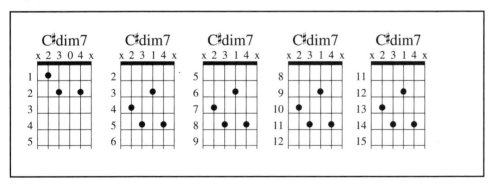

F♯min7♭5

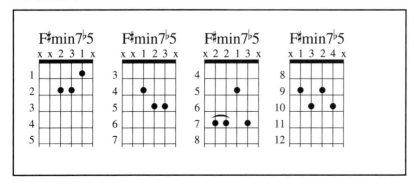

B Dominant Type

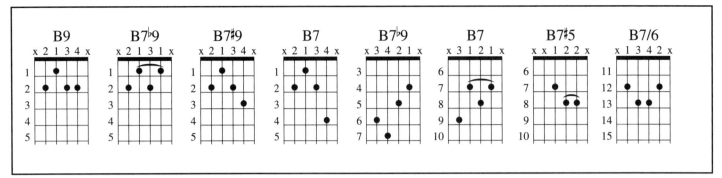

Amin7♭5

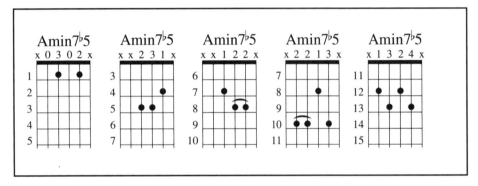

D Dominant Type

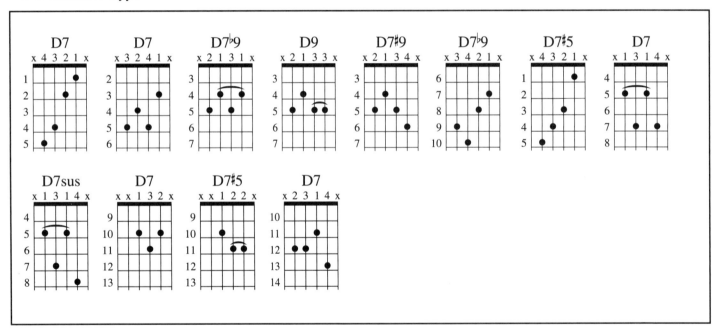

Dmin7♭5

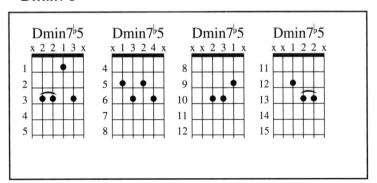

Region 6

C Major Type

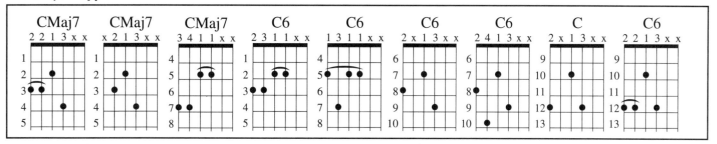

D Minor Type

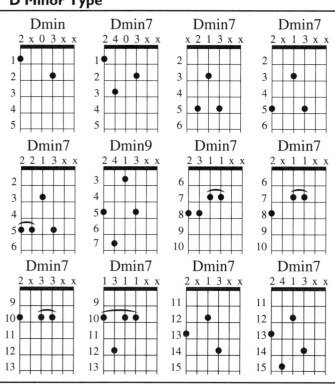

G Dominant Type

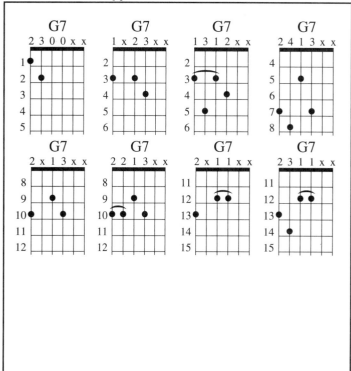

E Minor Type

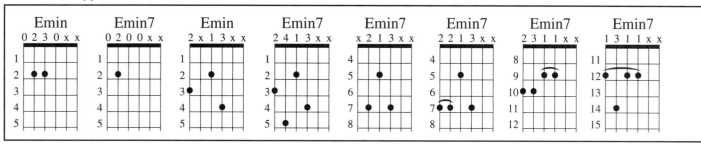

E♭dim7

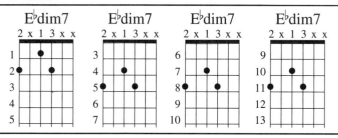

C♯dim7

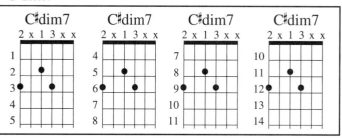

F♯min7♭5

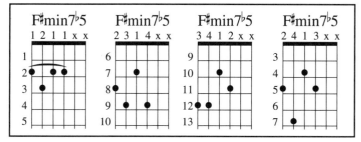

B Dominant Type

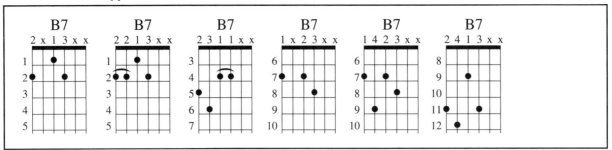

Amin7♭5

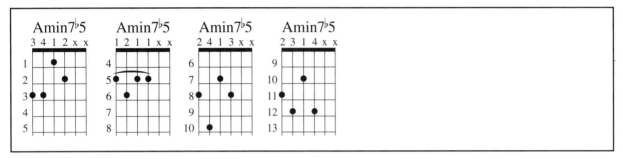

D Dominant Type

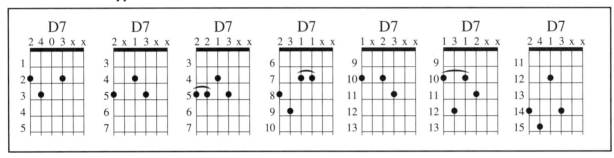

Dmin7♭5

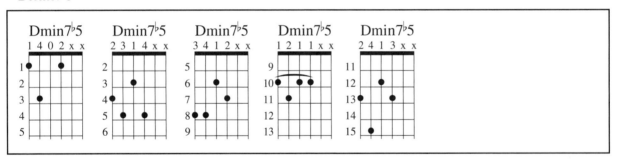

Whew! That's a lot of work. Yes it is, but remember that you will use many of these chords over and over in other songs you'll learn. This is a necessary step because you need a variety of chord voicings in many registers to play with style and taste. If you're always using the same chords in every song you play, things can start sounding a little stale. The concept of register is also very important. Generally, a good player strives for contrast in a group setting. If the soloist is playing in the upper registers, it is usually a good idea to accompany in the lower registers, and vice versa. Obviously, a sizable chord vocabulary is necessary to do this well. So now what?

Now, you need to practice playing various combinations of all these chords (or at least the ones you really like) within the context of our song. The following example shows one chorus of "I'm in the Mood for Love" using some of the chords we discovered in the last section.

The slash marks represent beats, not necessarily strums, although you certainly could strum "4 to the bar" as well, in which case you would strum once for each beat. On the CD that comes with this book, you may find that the strumming is handled in a somewhat random way if you're not used to listening to jazz. Instead of keeping strict time by strumming non-stop, chords are used as sort of "splashes" of color to complement the soloist. This is called "comping." This also means that you have to keep time internally along with listening to the other members of the group.

Become familiar with the chords below and then practice comping the chord changes while actually playing the song. When you can do that fairly well, try using different chords.

I'M IN THE MOOD FOR LOVE
(Comping Example)

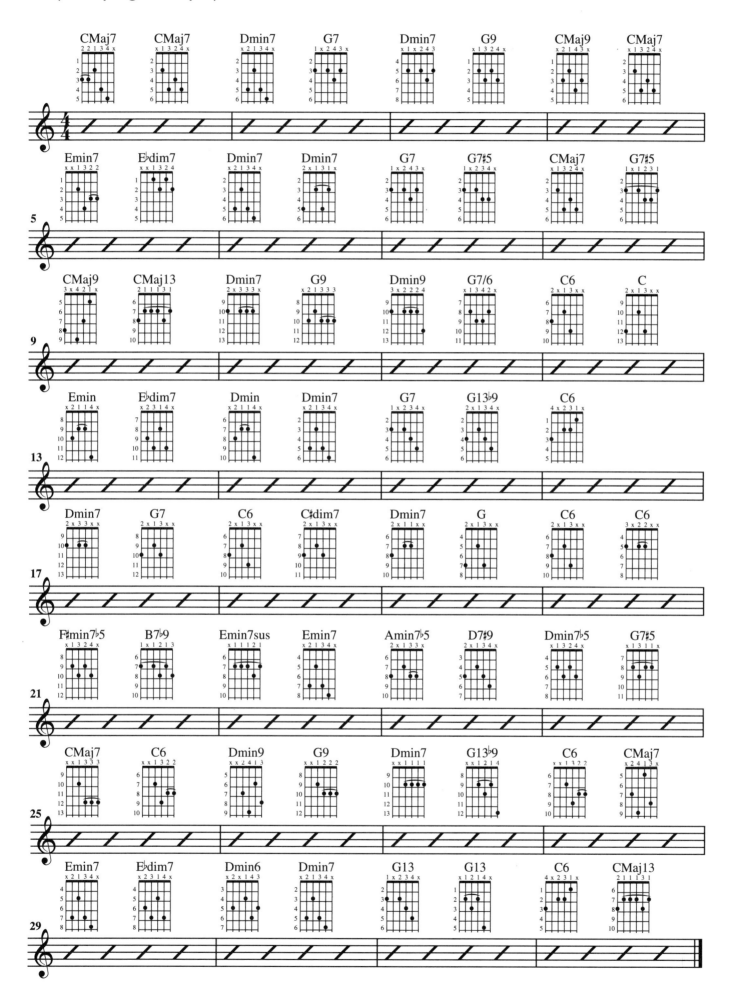

Chord Melody Style

At this point, you have the information (and with practice, the skills) to play "I'm in the Mood for Love" in single notes (in two different octaves), along with plenty of chords you can use to accompany others.

Now, let's think about playing this song in a *chord melody* style. What this means is that you will play the melody of the song using both single notes and chords. Chord melody playing is so deep that you could quite literally arrange and re-arrange almost any song for years and years to come. For our purposes, we'll discuss the basics.

After this, there is a basic chord melody arrangement of "I'm in the Mood for Love" to practice. While it is alright to learn a specific arrangement of a particular tune, many players who play in this style literally improvise a new arrangement for a song every time they play it. Improvising a chord melody performance requires a vast vocabulary of arranging techniques, a broad chord vocabulary and a true understanding of the fretboard. Yes, you can do this—but it does take a lot of practice and experience. For now, however, concentrate on fully understanding the basics.

Guidelines for Arranging

1. Generally, you will have to raise the melody an octave if you are learning the song from a book or sheet music. This will give you more strings to work with for harmonization. Once in a while, you may run across a song whose range spans two or more octaves. In that case, transposition may be impossible. Lower notes in the melody may have to be played as single notes, *diads* (two-note chords), or triads, saving full harmonization in the melody for notes in the middle and upper registers. For most songs, however, you'll just raise the entire melody one octave and things will work out just fine.

2. You may want to try transposing the song into a key other than the one in which it was written. It is often possible to create beautiful effects using open string voicings that another key may suggest.

3. Memorize the melody in single notes (which you have already done).

4. Memorize the chord changes and be able to play them all over the fretboard (you've already done that too).

5. Arrange the song with basic chords first. After you can do that proficiently, try to dress up the arrangement with chord enhancements and other arranging techniques, such as *substitutions* (replacing a chord as written with a different chord of similar function) and *passing chords* (non-diatonic chords inserted between diatonic chords to create a smooth progression).

6. Keep your arrangements loose. Eventually you'll want to improvise in this style. Constantly update and apply new skills to your repertoire.

Chord Melody Basics

Generally, the melody will be the highest note in a chord. Some players like to harmonize much of the melody and others prefer a lighter approach where chords are used more sparingly. By the same token, some players enjoy large, rich harmonies while others like to imply harmonies with smaller chords. It comes down to experience and taste. This section will touch upon some of the important key areas. *Mastering Jazz Guitar: Chord Melody* from the *Complete Jazz Guitar Method* and *The Art of Solo Guitar, Volumes 1 and 2* will help you dig deeper into this style of playing. Once you have the basics together, being a good chord melody player is really a matter of knowing many

different arranging techniques. Keep in mind that many of the techniques that are used in band and orchestral arrangements work equally well on the guitar.

The most basic skill to master is recognizing chord tones in the melody. This example shows the melody and basic chord changes in the first four bars of our song. Chord tones in the melody are indicated.

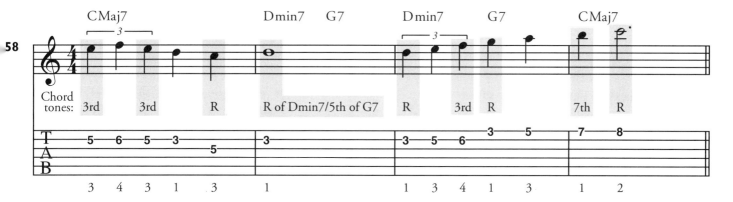

Below are two possible ways to harmonize the melody using some of the chords we discovered earlier. Notice that when we extend or alter some chords, more melody

notes can be used as chord tones. Remember that you don't have to harmonize every note.

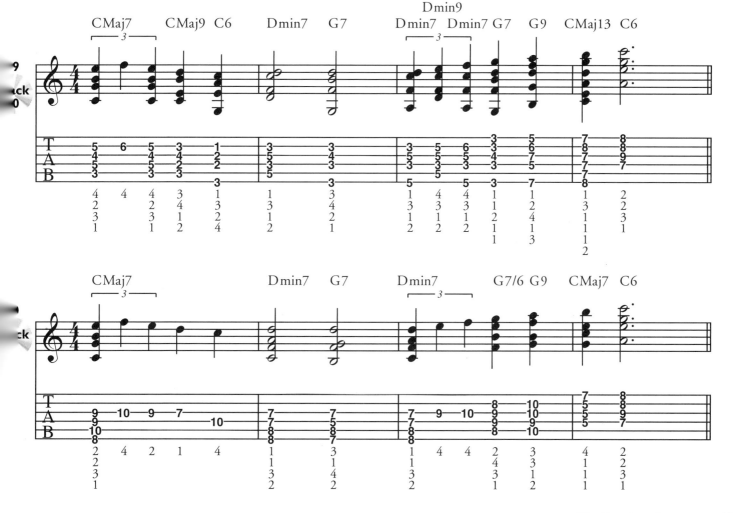

Using this same process, we could harmonize the entire
song like this:

I'M IN THE MOOD FOR LOVE
(Chord Melody)

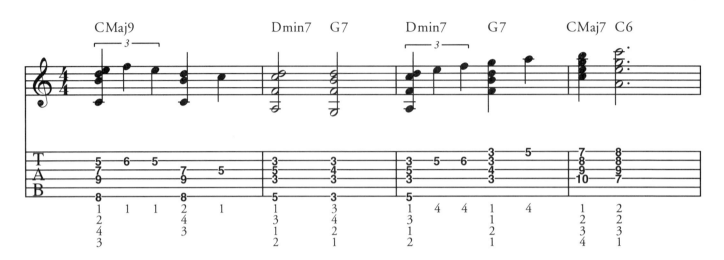

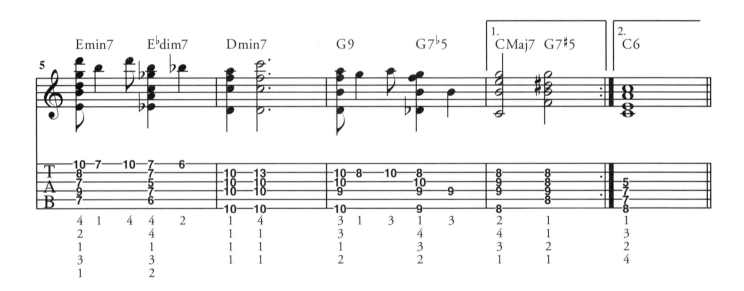

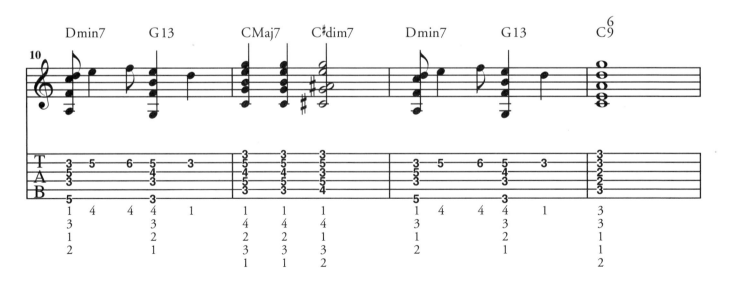

Learning to Improvise

Learning to improvise jazz is a lifelong pursuit. The goal is to translate the musical ideas from your head and your heart to your hands and your instrument. There is a lot to learn and a lot to practice. What you are doing, in effect, is learning how to use the elements of music to create spontaneous music on the guitar. You must know how to use the tools available for improvisation and you must know your way around the guitar.

After studying improvisation for a while, you will start to realize that experience is your best teacher. You can learn all about the tools, but working with those tools (a lot!) is the only way to become an accomplished improviser. You should realize that listening to a lot of improvised music is indispensable and possibly the single most important element in learning to improvise. Practicing improvisational techniques will only go so far. An intense amount of listening is the best way to learn how others apply these techniques and will therefore help you develop an improvisational style of your own.

The following is an overview of some of the tools we use for improvising.

Scales

While not the most important element of improvisation, scales are where most students begin. Learning to improvise with scales will get you up and running.

Here is a chart that shows various chord types and some of the scales that work well with them.

CHORD	FUNCTION	MAJOR OR MINOR KEY	SCALE OR MODE	STARTING ON
Maj6, Maj7	I or IV	Major	Major	Root of Chord
Maj9, Maj13	I or IV	Major	Major Pentatonic	Root of Chord
	I or IV	Major	Major Pentatonic	5th of Chord
	IV	Major	Major Pentatonic	9th of Chord
	IV	Major	Lydian	Root of Chord
Maj7	VI	Minor	Lydian #2	Root of Chord
Dom7, 9, 11, 13, 7sus4 (except where marked *)	Any	Major	Major Pentatonic	Root of Chord
	Any	Major	Major Pentatonic	4th of Chord
	Any	Major	Minor Pentatonic	Root of Chord
	Any	Major	Minor Pentatonic	5th of Chord
	Any	Major	Blues	Root of Chord
	Any	Major	Mixolydian	Root of Chord
	IV	Minor	Lydian ♭7* (not good for 11 or sus 4 chords)	Root of Chord
	V	Minor	Mixolydian ♭6* (not good for 13th chords)	Root of Chord
	V	Minor	Phrygian Dominant* (not good for 9 chords)	Root of Chord
7sus4 Chords	Any	Both	Dorian	Root of Chord
	Any	Both	Dorian	5th of Chord
Dom7♭5	Any	Both	Whole Tone	Root, 3rd, ♭5, ♭7 of Chord
9♭5	Any	Both	WH Diminished	½ Step above Root
	Any	Both	Lydian ♭7	Root of Chord
	Any	Both	Super Locrian	Root of Chord
	Any	Both	Blues	Root of Chord
Dom7♯5	Any	Both	Whole Tone	Root, 3rd, ♭7 of Chord
9♯5	Any	Both	Mixolydian ♭6	Root of Chord
	Any	Both	Phrygian Dom	Root of Chord
	Any	Both	Super Locrian	Root of Chord
Dom7♭9, 13♭9, 7♯9	Any	Both	WH Diminished	Root, 3rd, 5th, ♭7, ♭9 of Chord
	Any	Both	Super Locrian	Root of Chord
	Any	Both	Phrygian Dominant* (not good for 7♯9 chord)	Root of Chord
7♯9	Any	Both	Minor Pentatonic	Root of Chord
	Any	Both	Blues	Root of Chord
	Any	Both	Dorian	Root of Chord
Min6, 9 11, 13	ii or vi	Major	Minor Pentatonic	Root of Chord
	ii	Major	Dorian	Root of Chord
	iv	Minor	Lydian♭3♭7	Root of Chord
	vi	Major	Natural Minor	Root of Chord

A person could get dizzy looking at charts like this. Some students get completely obsessed with learning and memorizing scales and applications. This is not necessary. As stated earlier, as you mature as an improviser, you actually depend less on scales and more on some of the other tools. Still, looking over and using some of these scale applications can give you a good overview of chord/scale relationships. You don't want to become "a walking encyclopedia of scales looking for a chord to collide with."

Arpeggios

Arpeggios are one of your best improvisation tools. They are the path through any chord progression. Regardless of the other tools you may like to use, arpeggios spell out the chord changes and give you the kind of control you need in an improvised setting.

If you are accustomed to using scales as your primary vehicle for improvisation, you have no doubt noticed that sometimes you hit notes that, while in an appropriate scale, just don't sound that great. This is usually because you have played a non-chord tone on a strong (accented) beat in the measure.

Here's the deal. You should be able to hear the chord changes in your solo even if there is no chord accompaniment being played behind you. The easiest way to accomplish this is by starting your melodic phrases on the tones in the chord being played.

Here's another thing. The most important notes you play are the chord tones. When you choose to improvise using a particular scale, all you are really doing is deciding what notes you want to surround your chord tones with. It is simply choosing what kind of color tones to add to your arpeggios.

The following examples show different lines you can play against a G7 chord. In each case the chord tones are really defining the tonality of the chord. The other notes in the line give the melody its character.

Here, we see the G7 arpeggio tones in conjunction with
a C Major scale (Mixolydian mode).

Now, let's look at G7 arpeggio tones in conjunction with
a G♯ Diminished scale.

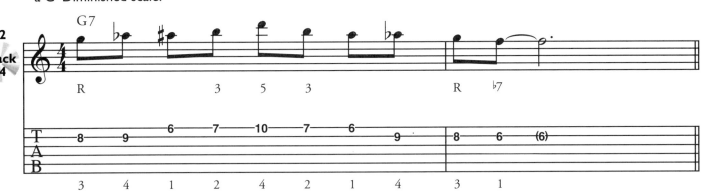

Finally, let's look at G7 arpeggio tones in conjunction with
the G Super Locrian scale.

So, you can see that the arpeggio tones give you the inside tonality needed to establish the chord, and the scale gives your lines their "spark" or character.

How do you develop this skill in your playing? At first, improvise using only chord tones. This helps you find the path through the chord progression. As you do this, you'll find the content of the solo to be rather bland.

That's alright because once you are comfortable with the "path," you'll find it easier to incorporate the scales. Of course, this means finding the correct arpeggios all over the fretboard. Again, this is a good thing because you will use all these arpeggios over and over again in most of the songs you'll ever learn.

Here is a sample solo over the changes to "I'm in the
Mood for Love" using only arpeggio tones.

I'M IN THE MOOD FOR LOVE
(Solo Using Only Arpeggio Tones)

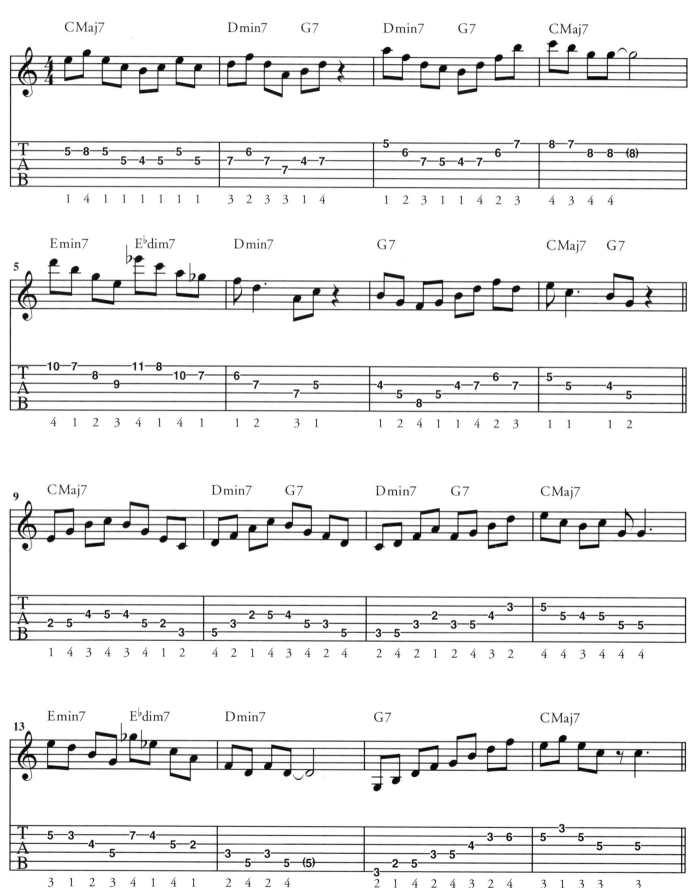

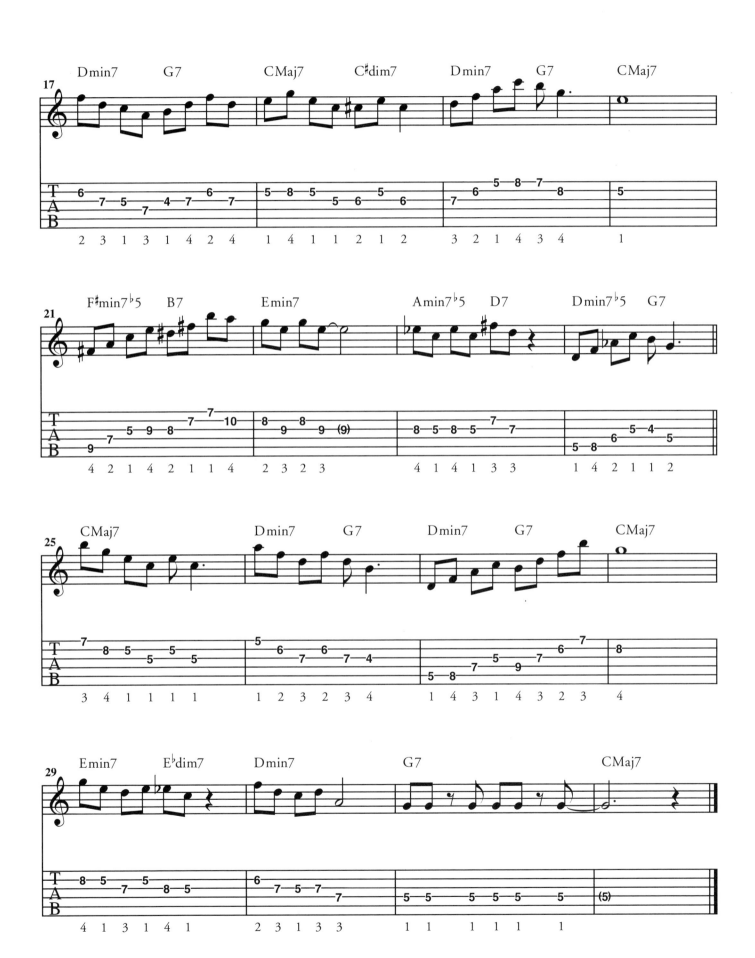

Melodic Patterns

You might have thought that melodic patterns were just a way to practice scales and exercise your fingers, but they are really great improvisational devices in their own right.

Probably their most important aspect is that they fill your head with melodic possibilities that you wouldn't necessarily come up with on your own. These ideas, over time, blend with other tools and become part of your voice as an improviser. Imagine all the possibilities that would exist if you were to learn 20 or 30 melodic patterns with your favorite scales.

Using melodic patterns to connect two or more shorter ideas is a great way to lengthen your melodic lines. The following examples illustrate this idea.

P
⌢ = *Pull-off.*
Technique where you pull off from a higher note on the fretboard to a lower note, picking only the first note.

Chord Superimposition

Chord superimposition refers to playing an arpeggio of a particular chord over an entirely different chord. This concept can be extremely simple, but some players have used this idea in very advanced ways. The next example shows how you can play simple diatonic arpeggios over different chords from the same scale.

Playing an Emin7 arpeggio over a CMaj7 chord implies a CMaj9 sound.

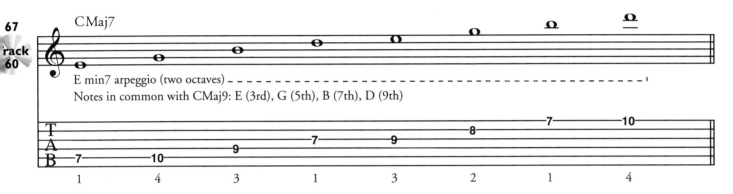

Playing an FMaj7 arpeggio over a Dmin7 chord implies a Dmin9 sound.

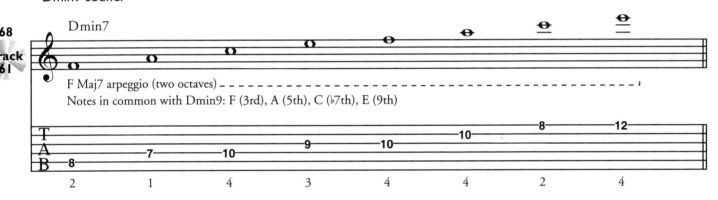

Playing an Amin7 arpeggio over an FMaj7 chord implies an FMaj9 sound.

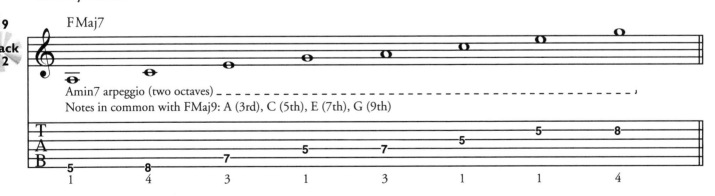

Playing an E Major arpeggio over a G dominant chord implies a G13♭9 sound.

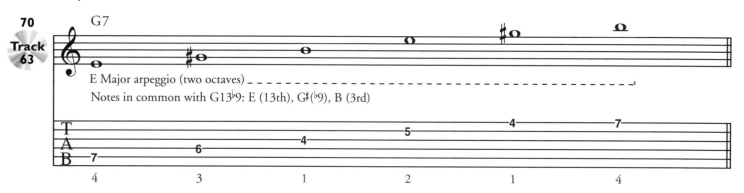

Playing an A♭dim7 arpeggio over a G7 chord implies a G7♭9 sound.

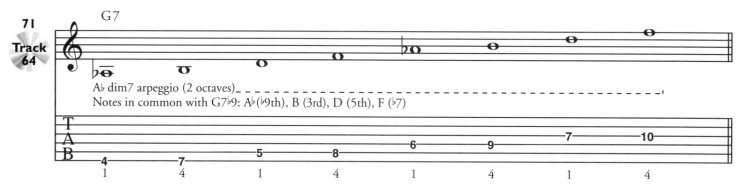

The idea here is to experiment and see what cool ideas you come up with. It takes a little patience, but finding a unique sound that you discovered yourself is a great payoff.

Licks

The whole point of improvisation is to express the musical lines you hear in your head and execute them on your instrument. The best moments are when you get "lost" in the process, freely creating without conscious thought. These "states of grace" don't happen all the time. Sometimes the intellectual use of all your tools keeps you afloat instead. This is normal for all players. Licks are one tool most players depend on from time to time. Licks are preconceived ideas that an improviser knows will work over certain chords or chord progressions. You can consider licks as part of your overall vocabulary. Obviously, improvising is a lot more than just stringing your favorite licks together. Still, they do serve an important function.

The best source of licks is recorded music. When you hear a phrase you like, stop the recording and learn the lick. Then, figure out various applications for that lick. You'll find most licks will work over many kinds of chords and chord progressions. Other good sources for licks are the many "lick books" that are available and transcriptions of actual jazz solos. Of course, doing your own transcribing (listening to music and writing it out in music notation) has many benefits, including improving your ear and helping you to become proficient at writing music notation.

Following are some sample licks to apply in your own solos. Be sure you practice them in all keys.

H⌢ = Hammer-on.
Technique where you hammer-on from a lower note on the fretboard to a higher note on the fretboard, picking only the first note.

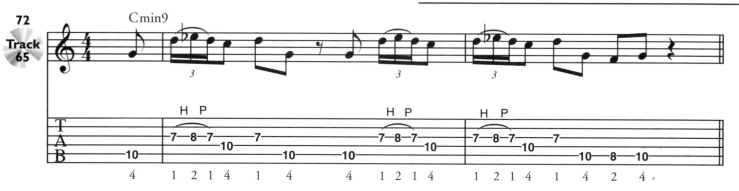

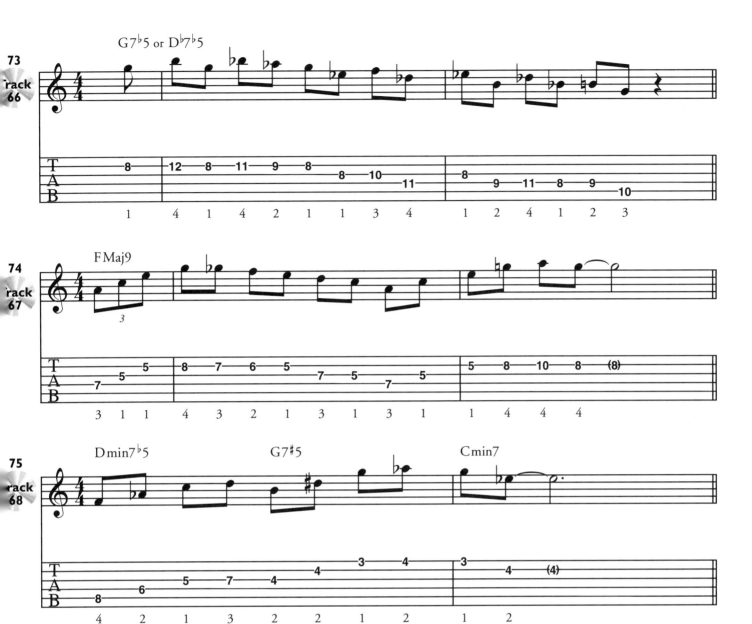

Spontaneous Ideas

These are the moments we all wait for. This is the main reward. Nothing feels quite like it. Nothing can be quite so elusive, and you can't fake it or force it. Knowing your material well and staying relaxed can set the stage for these moments of inspiration. Self-consciousness is the enemy. Try…but not too hard.

Putting It All Together and a Few Words About Improvised Examples

As mentioned earlier, learning to improvise takes some knowledge and practice. The tools that have been discussed so far are really just the tip of the iceberg. Each one takes on profound implications after working with it over time. It can't really be explained; it has to be experienced. Also realize that there are more tools; I have recommended a few other books (see page 5) so you can dive into this material more deeply.

The next example is an "improvised" solo using many of the tools discussed previously in this book. It should be noted that this solo is not really improvised. Rather, it is composed and worked out to illustrate the usage of the techniques so far discussed. It does get the point across, but lacks the spirit and spontaneity of a true improvisational experience. While you may find material in this solo that you choose to use in your own solos, it is important to realize that that the purpose of this solo is not to give you dozens of "hot licks." It simply shows an academic application of the theory and techniques you've covered on these pages.

We'll start out with a solo over the changes to "I'm in the Mood for Love." The rest of the book consists of tunes shown in the following ways:

1. In single notes spanning one octave—it will be up to you to learn the same melody an octave higher or lower.

2. A sample chord chart showing useable chord shapes all over the six regions discussed earlier.

3. A sample chord melody treatment of the tune.

4. A sample "improvised" solo.

Feel free to experiment with techniques such as pull-offs
and hammer-ons in the solos that follow.

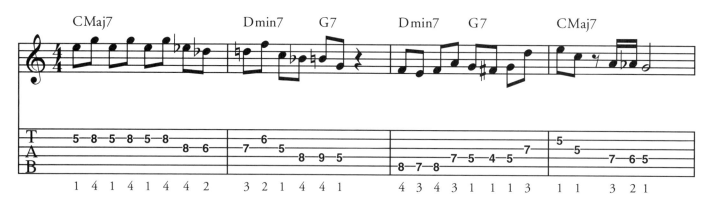

I'm in the Mood for Love

Track
69

("Improvised" Solo)

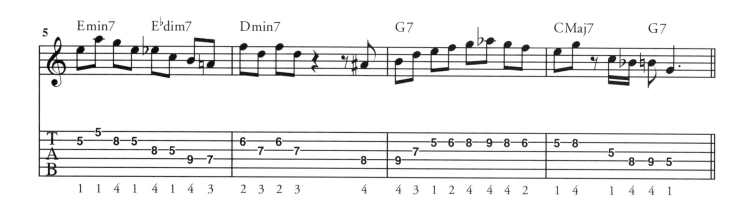

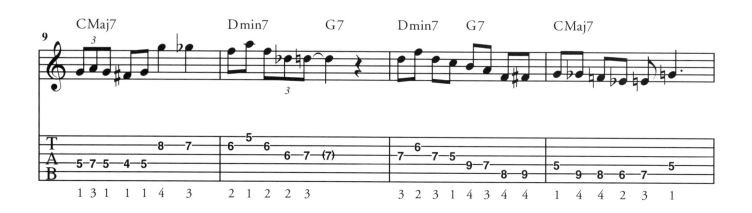

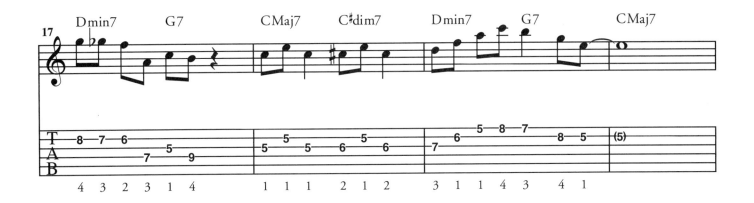

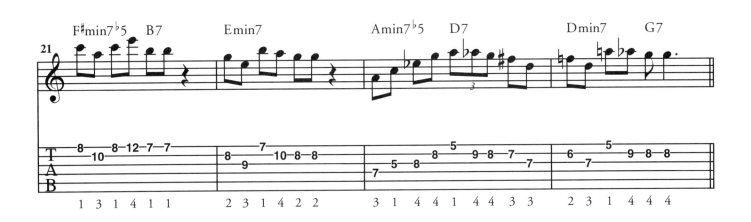

Chapter 18: "Over the Rainbow"

Over the Rainbow

(Melody in Single Notes)

Harburg/Arlen

* This chord has a D♭ which clashes with the D in the melody. It is standard, however, to use this chord as accompaniment when another musician is soloing.

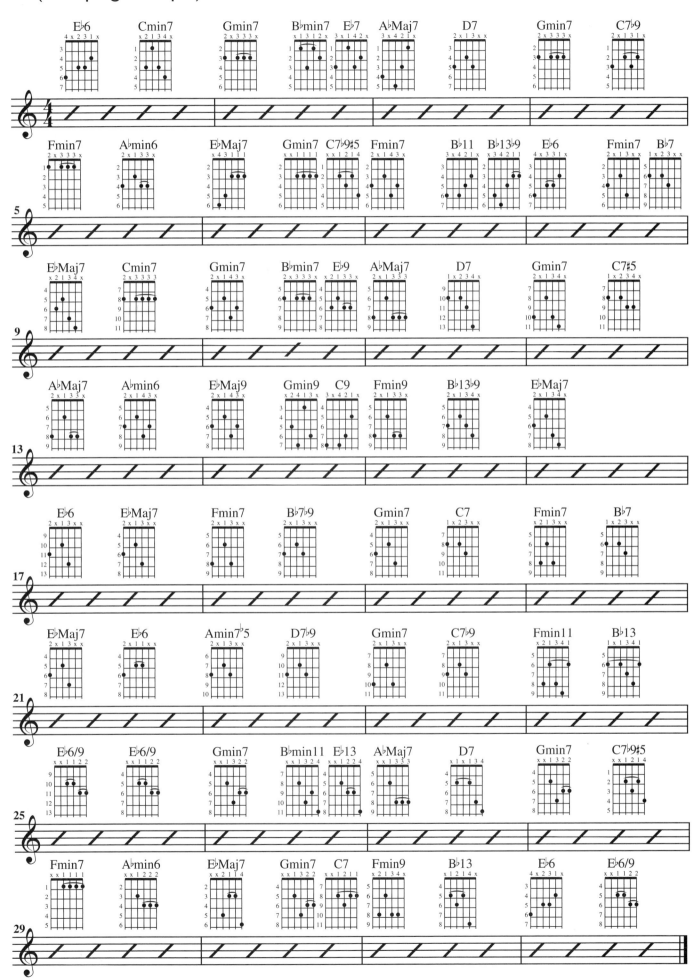

OVER THE RAINBOW
(Chord Melody)

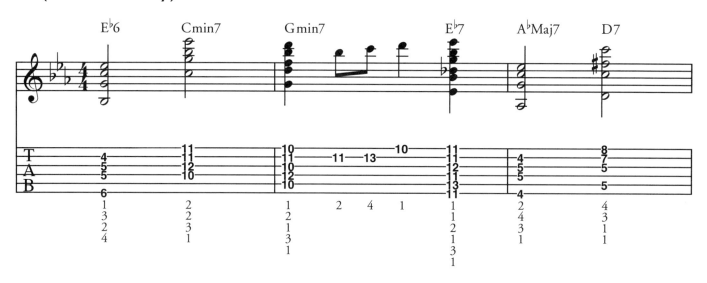

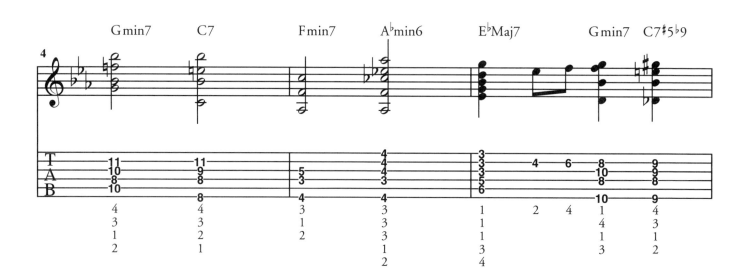

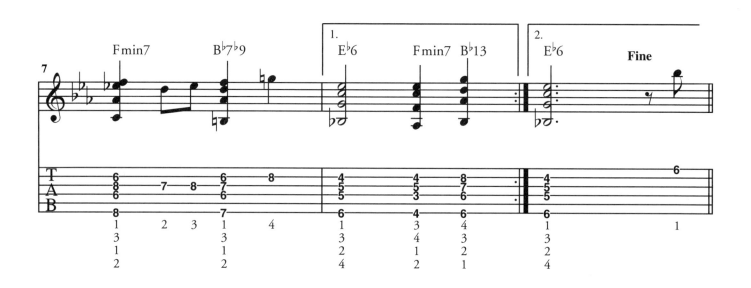

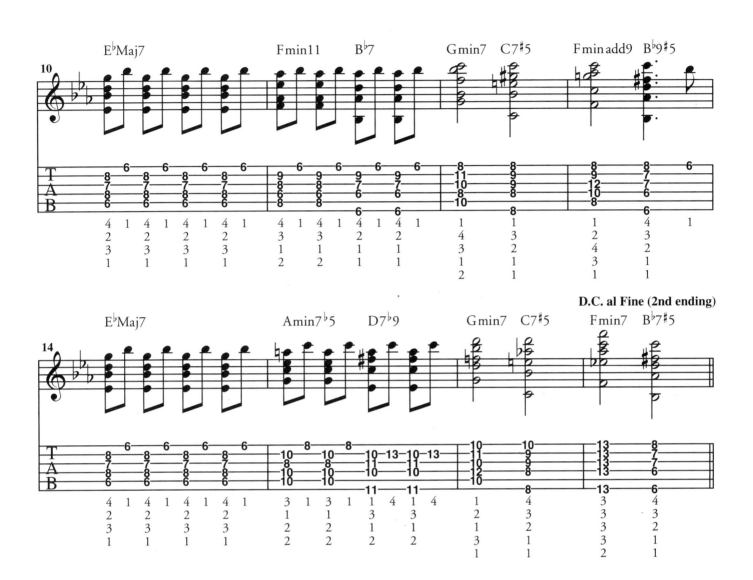

Over the Rainbow

("Improvised" Solo)

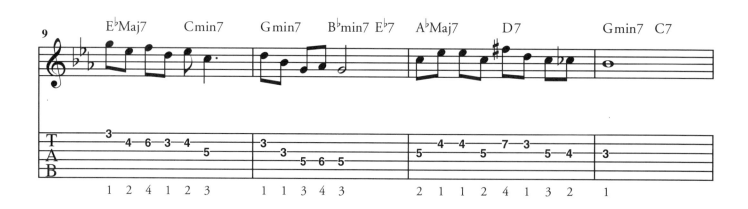

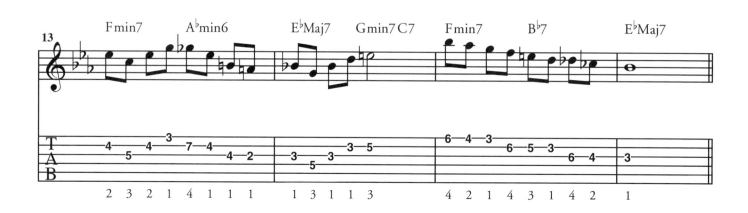

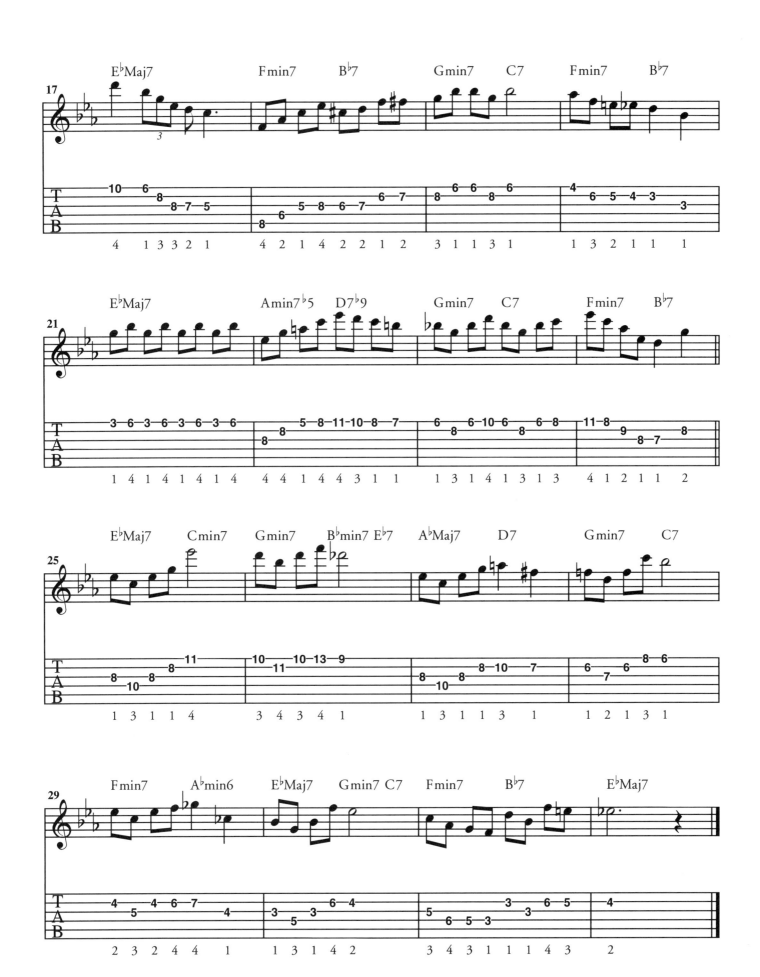

Chapter 19: "Blue Moon"

BLUE MOON

(Melody in Single Notes)

Rodgers/Hart

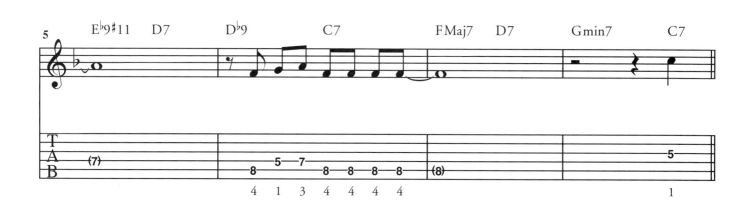

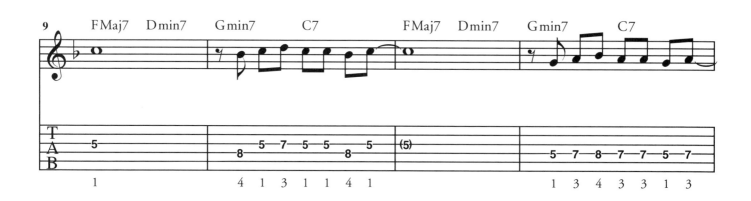

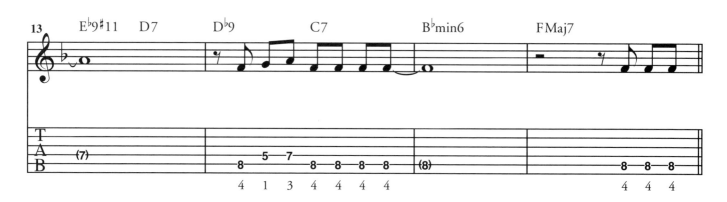

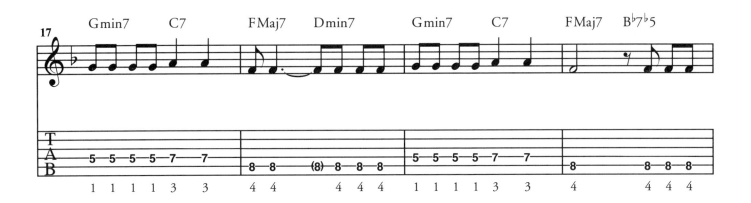

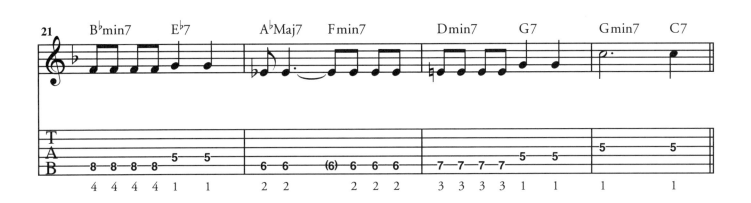

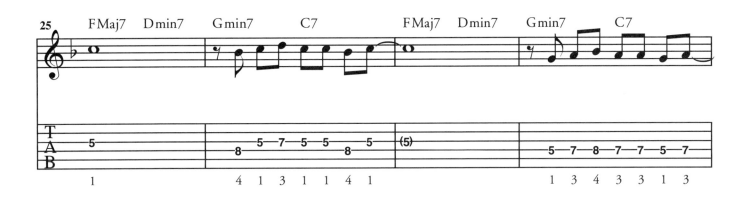

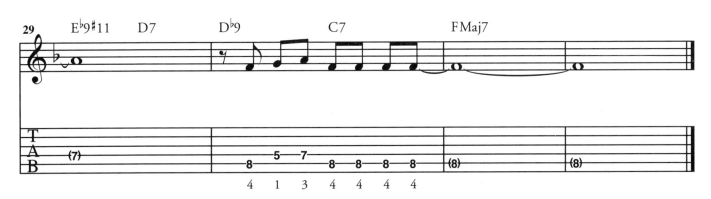

BLUE MOON
(Comping Example)

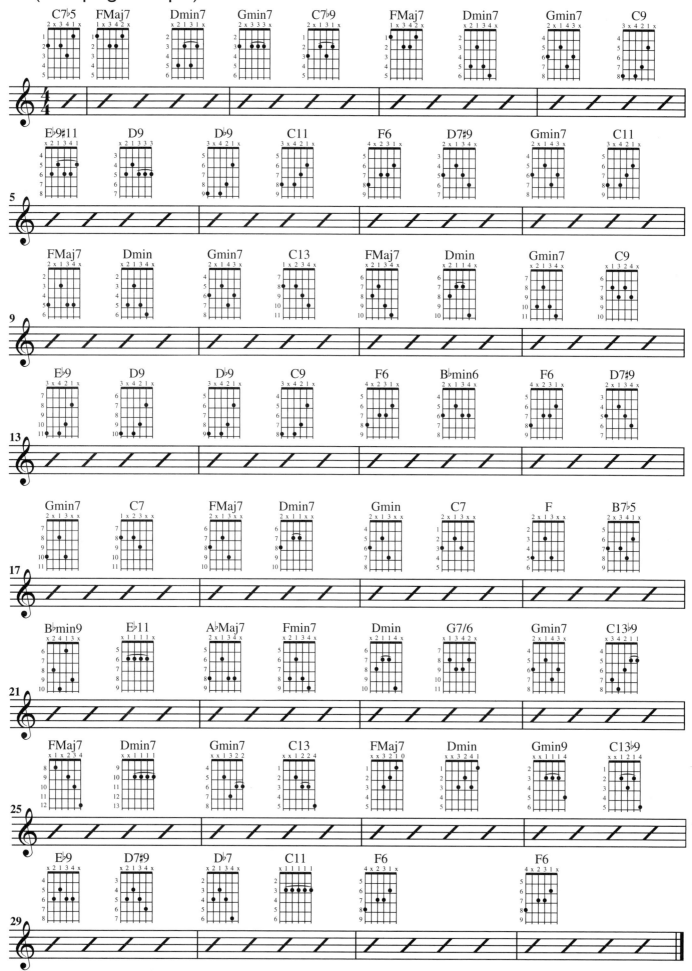

BLUE MOON
(Chord Melody)

Blue Moon
("Improvised" Solo)

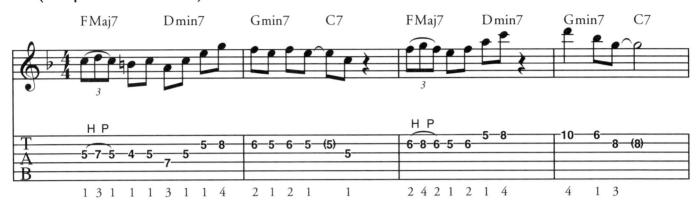

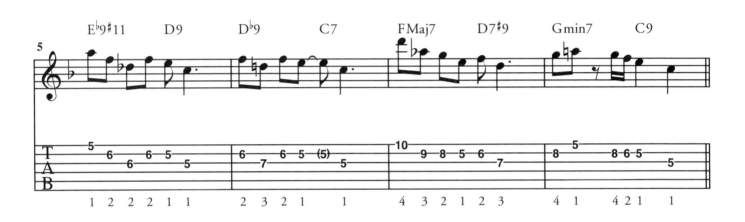

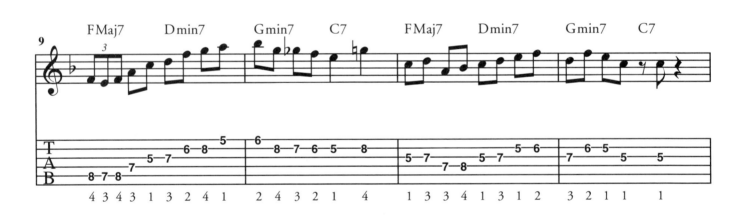

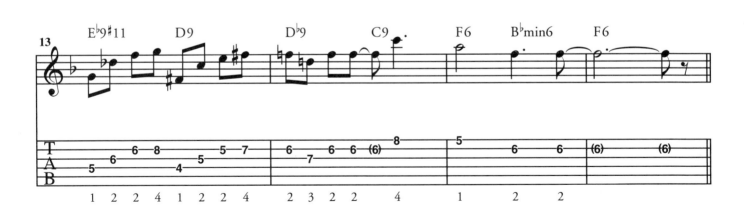

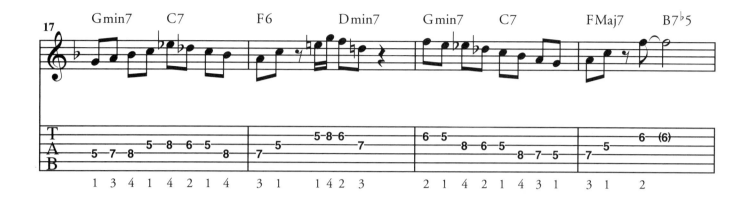

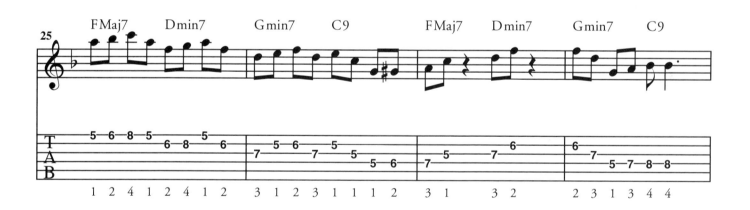

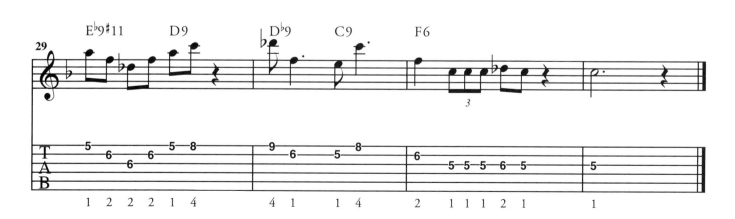

Chapter 20: The Blues and Rhythm Changes

Besides all the great standards and jazz tunes that have been written, there are two more categories of songs you should be aware of: the blues and rhythm changes. Basically, these are two different types of chord progressions that jazz musicians through the years have found to be particularly enjoyable to play. As a result, hundreds of songs have been written using these chord changes. Both the blues and rhythm changes have countless variations based on a basic set of chord changes. Since you will undoubtedly learn many songs that consist of these progressions, it would be a good idea to gain some familiarity with them. Entire books have been written about these two forms. The following examples are simply an introduction.

The Blues

Blues progressions are based on a 12-measure form using a typical I–IV–V7 progression, which you may have played in a more basic form.

Basic 12-Bar Blues

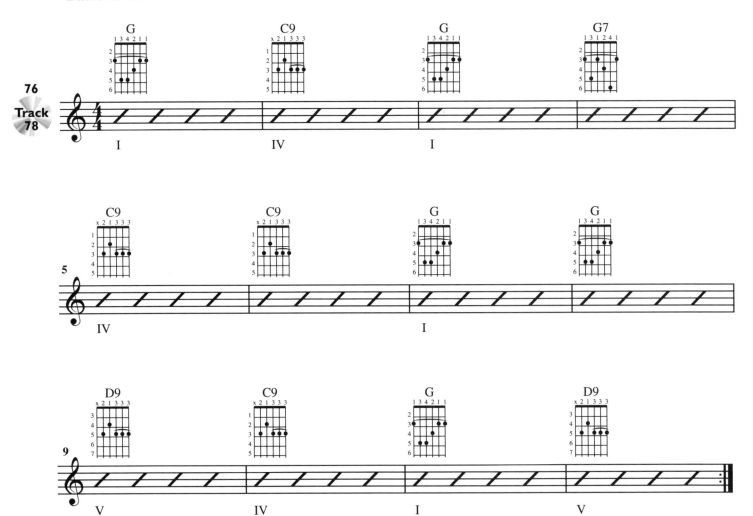

Jazz musicians usually beef up the basic progression with
ii–V7–I progressions, chord substitutions and passing
chords. Here are some jazzier examples:

Jazz Blues Variation 1

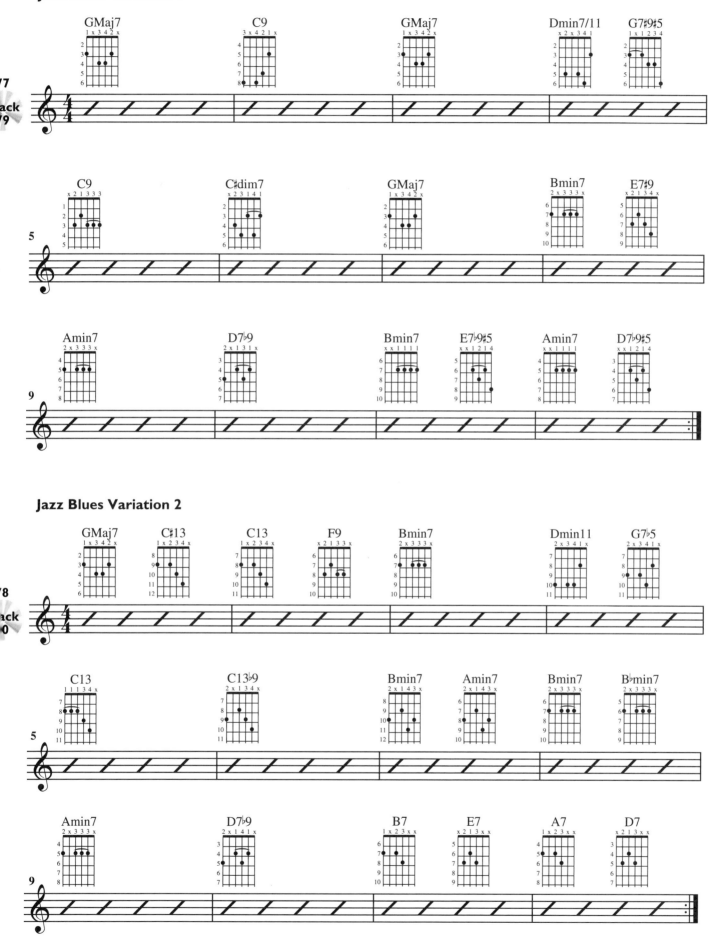

Jazz Blues Variation 2

Rhythm Changes

Rhythm changes are a 32-bar form in which the A sections are built around a I–vi–ii–V7 progression (a ii–V7–I–♭ii dim progression beginning in measure 5 is often thrown in for variation). The B section flows through the cycle of 4ths starting a major third above the song's tonic.

Here are the most basic rhythm changes:

Rhythm Changes

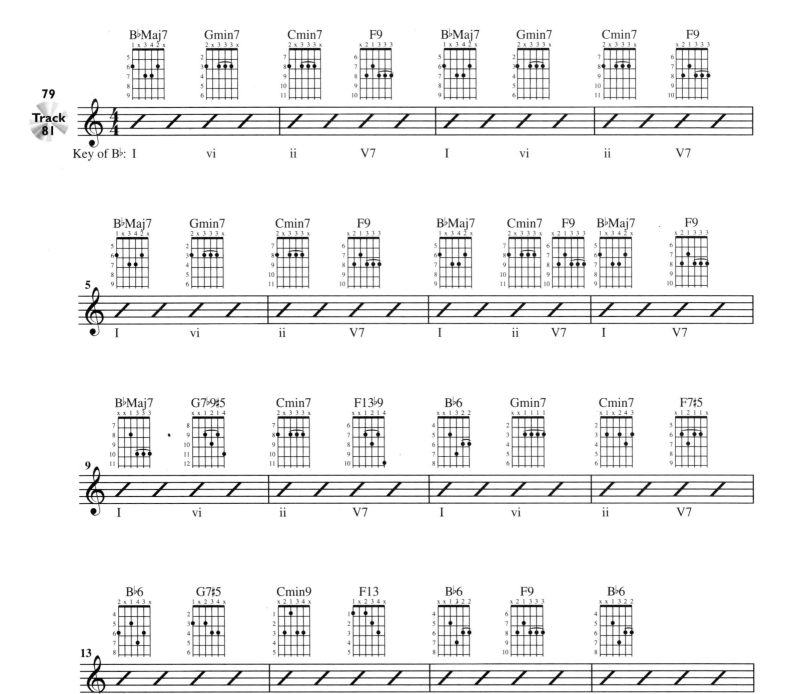

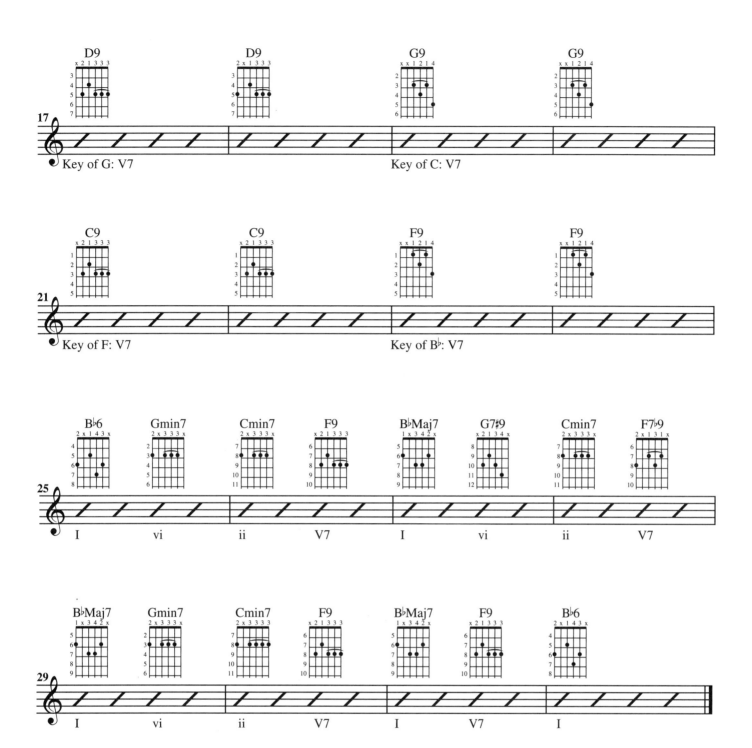

Key of G: V7

Key of C: V7

Key of F: V7

Key of B♭: V7

I   vi   ii   V7   I   vi   ii   V7

I   vi   ii   V7   I   V7   I

CONCLUSION

Congratulations, you've made it through *The Total Jazz Guitarist*. You now have the tools you need to play melodies, comp chord changes and improvise your own solos. Now, all you need is lots and lots of practice. Use the methods in this book to learn new tunes. You'll find that learning the basics of each new tune gets a little easier. When you need a break from practicing, listen as much as you can to the masters of jazz, both live and recorded performances. Jazz is an endless journey, so keep challenging yourself and never stop learning.